Reflections Through Time and Rhyme

A collection of original poems on Childhood, Bucks County, Christmas, Family Ties, Life Lines, Pathways, Seascapes, Summertime, The Inner Child, Wings and Wintertime

by

Sharon E. Licht

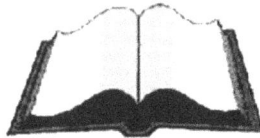

CCB Publishing
British Columbia, Canada

Reflections Through Time and Rhyme: A collection of original poems on Childhood, Bucks County, Christmas, Family Ties, Life Lines, Pathways, Seascapes, Summertime, The Inner Child, Wings, and Wintertime

Copyright ©2011 by Sharon E. Licht
ISBN-13   978-1-926918-62-4
First Edition

Library and Archives Canada Cataloguing in Publication
Licht, Sharon E., 1945-
Reflections through time and rhyme : a collection of original poems on childhood, Bucks County, Christmas, family ties, life lines, pathways, seascapes, summertime, the inner child, wings, and wintertime / written by Sharon E. Licht.
Poems.
ISBN 978-1-926918-62-4
I. Title.
PS3612.I34R43 2011   811'.6   C2011-903624-X

Publisher: CCB Publishing
              British Columbia, Canada
              www.ccbpublishing.com

Dedication

For my Father, Charles T. Bleasdale, Sr., and my Mother,
Ethel Bale Bleasdale, who have earned their wings in heaven.

For my Husband, Jeffrey, who has been supportive of my
endeavors over the years.

For my children, Kristin and Jeremy and their spouses,
Joseph and Lisa, my grandchildren, Nicole, Ford, Gavin, Layla
and great-grandson Leon; you are my shining lights.

For my Sister, Carole, Brother, Charles and their families with love.

Contents

Childhood

Back to Bucks County

Christmastime

Family Ties

Life Lines

Pathways

Seascapes

Summertime

The Inner Child

Wings

Wintertime

CHILDHOOD

There lives a distant sunbeam
Peeking through my memories….

A Distant Sunbeam

There lives a distant sunbeam
Peeking through my memories,
Lighting up my wondrous dream
From a far away shimmering sea.

There rests a glistening drop of dew,
Gleaming where the tall grass grew,
Calling a child I once knew,
Singing sweet songs in the meadow for you.

Grown in a field, dandelion weeds,
Blown on winds from little seeds,
A young child pulls a buttercup in,
Reflecting its light on another's chin.

Perchance to chase a butterfly
With silky wings to fly up high;
Perchance to catch a drifting dragonfly,
Or to launch a kite with one easy try.

There shines your own personal star,
Sparkling over that land afar,
Reach out; catch your very own dream,
Suspended out there on a blue moonbeam.

Call the child that was left back there,
The child with the wind-blown hair.
Run through the rays of the distant sun,
You are that child. Take time to become one.

A Journey with Father

Standing in father's work shoes, wearing his big work hat,
Folks called me "Little Charlie", I was so proud of that!
Running errands on weekends, the shadow of my Dad,
I was his only daughter, not a son, boy, or lad.

We drove up to the feed mill for food for our hens and dogs,
A rambling old barn that was, with hay for cows and hogs.
The old mill smelled of sawdust with wooden floors that creaked,
A large barn full of old must, and high-hipped roof that leaked.

Two old men worked the feed store; they had a dozen cats,
Sneaking through the feed bins, hunting for mice and scraps!
The feed mill was a remnant, leftover from the past,
A ghost from the eighteen hundreds; of its kind, the last.

There was a gold cash register, an old-time machine,
I watched in wide-eyed wonder, keys pushed by fingers lean.
The two old men were brothers, who worked the feed mill store,
Wearing gray stripped train hats; clinking coins in their cash drawer.

Loose feed filled paper sacks; we tucked them under our arms,
Brown bags full and firmly packed with time and hometown charm.
The feed mill store long torn down: empty space stands in its place,
    And thoughts of a loving father, —
        Those, time cannot erase.

Another Time

Rocking chairs rocking, small children in stockings;
Time keeps on knocking on the doors of my heart.
Teddy bears sit gazing, old bears are amazing,
    Propped up on pillows of yellow daffodils.

Another time, a nursery rhyme
    Running up the clock.
A mouse is loose with Mother Goose,
    Hickory, Dickory and Dock!

How could there be an old man in the moon?
Did he fly up there in a colored balloon?
Rose colored memories linger with me today,
They sweep me away to hickory stick days.

Another time, a nursery rhyme
    Running up the clock,
A mouse is loose with Mother Goose,
    Hickory, Dickory and Dock, Dock, Dock!

Backyard Boundaries

As I look back, I look within
To backyard memories of bygone kin,
To sway on swings 'neath apple trees,
In backyards sweet with honeybees.

My childhood memories linger there,
In Bucks County where days are fair,
Where smells of freshly laundered clothes
Hang from lines where soft breezes blow.

The bed sheets flap and billow free
Blown on clothes lines hung from trees—
A happy place where children squeal
At the prospect of pole, line and reel.

My memories climb in backyard trees
With bygone relatives sailing free,
From boundaries drawn by lives of toil,
In vegetable gardens rich with soil.

As I look back, I look within;
I see sweat glistening on work-worn skin,
Soil-caked hands tending sweet corn rows
With wood-handled rakes and garden hoes.

A back stooped over the strawberry patch,
A cigarette dangling, lit with a match,
A lawn mower whirling through blades of grass,
Fueled by sweat not by gallons of gas.

When I look back, I look within
To sweet old memories of long-gone kin,
To firefly lights in mosquito nights,
To summertime when all was right.

Where lightening bugs in Mason jars
Took precedence over journeys afar.
My memories are back; they've taken me in
To backyard boundaries—
    Lovely within...

Big Ted's Red Wagon

Climb into your red wagon, Big Ted,
I'll take you for a grand ride instead.
Get ready for some fun
In the early morning sun,
Climb up into your wagon, Big Ted!

Get ready; get set; it's time to go,
I'll whisper a secret you should know.
Our neighbor, Mrs. Fox,
Is peeking through her window box
Get ready; get set; on with the show!

Sit down in your red wagon, Big Ted,
Don't fall out and bump your fuzzy head.
Buckle up your safety strap,
Make it snug across your lap,
Then you won't fall on your Teddy Bear head.

Bumpety-bump!

Bring Me a Moonbeam

Bring me a moonbeam, show me a sunbeam,
Shower me with dewdrops to hold in my hand.
Present me with a rosebud, a sweet smelling rosebud,
I'll shower you with precious gifts of life eternally.

Show me a bright smile; a laugh goes the extra mile,
Heart-to-heart in grand style is what is good for me.
Weave me a flower ring, blooming in the days of spring,
Wear a joyful heart that sings; these are such lovely things.

Falling little raindrops; catch them up like gumdrops,
Raining down for you and me as if they were candy.
These are small precious things; they make your heart sing.
These little gifts from up above are things I'm dreaming of.

Bring me a moonbeam,
    Shower me with sunbeams,
        Appreciate the little things —
        Moonbeams are free.

Chalk Lines

I've discovered a scar on my right pinky finger
From Jacks played on sidewalks where memories linger.
I loved to play Jacks by the hour as a child,
And bounce the red ball with flourish and style.

I've discovered the grid of the old Hopscotch lines
Drawn in white chalk, a schoolgirls' design.
Squares drawn were three singles, then, two, one, and two,
Marked one through eight is what we girls would do.

Then there was Stone School played on the front steps,
Which palm of your friend hides the stone; can you guess?
We passed through the grades one step at a time,
These young games were fun; they filled our pastime.

As I study the scar on my small pinky finger,
I'm drawn back in time where my memories linger,
While my inner child reflects on a token we'd find,
Perfect for tossing in Hopscotch chalk lines!

Childhood Travels

Behold a fair and fabled land,
Where beauty sleeps and castles climb.
Take hold, dear friend, my beckoning hand;
Fling wide the creaking doors of time.

'Tis there, old bear, our hearts revive,
Along old trails of dusty gray.
Take care; keep childhood dreams alive
In heart and home of yesterday.

Perhaps we'll rest our childlike chins
On windowsills of other times,
Perhaps we'll see a weathered face
Reflected in a childhood rhyme.

If we could brush the meadows bright
With colors hewn from apple-red,
We could escape on winged delight
And put our ticking fears to bed.

The truth lives in a spiral's rise
Forsaken long like sunken ships;
In dreams revived of castles high,
In passing tides of innocence.

Daddy Dear

"How much do you love me?"
I chirped from daddy's knee.
"A bushel basketful", he smiled,
And laughed endearingly.

"How much do you love me, child?"
Returned young daddy dear.
"Two bushel basketsful", I cried,
"I love you more, you see".

"I love you more".
He loved me most,
"I'll love you last";
He loved me first.

Our little game went on and on
Gaily, through the years,
Until dear father went away
In a basketful of tears.

Daddy's Shoes

I wish I could have known when I sat in Daddy's lap,
And the many happy days he put me in to nap,
One day those times would fly in the twinkling of an eye,
And looking back, I would reflect, on those rosy skies.

I wish I could have known, when I sat on Daddy's knee,
My young world was temporary; then I did not see.
I remember when we danced, and I stood on Daddy's shoes,
Small arms wrapped around his hips, as through the room we flew.

Two shadows on the wall; one tall, the other one small,
Such a young man was he, twenty-three, that's all!
Memories linger still, of climbing up on Daddy's back,
He was my handsome horse, as we galloped 'round the track.

Hear the clicking sound of Daddy's tongue against his teeth,
The whinnying cry he made to a playhouse horse hoof-beat!
Skipping around the floor, hanging on around his neck,
Laughing, giggling aloud, this girl gave Dad's cheek a peck.

I wish I could have known growing old and, somehow, grown,
Meant memories would go on after childhood days had flown.
While sitting here today, if back then I only knew,
My fondest memory would be dancing on Daddy's shoes.

Down By the Streambed

Down by the streambed dried up in the hot sun,
Digging for some molding clay where water used to run.
See the little children piling mounds of damp sand,
Making small creations near honeysuckle land.

Digging with their fingers underneath a silly tree,
Running up the sliding hill and laughing happily.
All the little children underneath the silly tree,
Poking feathers in their hair in a tent teepee.

Down by the streambed, painting faces, having fun,
Cowboys and Indians where water used to run,
Drumming on their tom-toms; Palomino pony rides,
Wooing in a winding stream where waters once ran high.

Foundations

My ancestors, recently, have called me
Backward in time to another reality,
Back to childhood, where my dreams grew,
Built in the life that I once knew.

Years have passed by, and my family's ghosts
Have made a pact with a heavenly host,
Lifting the veil on times long past.
I'll tell their story, as they ask.

A slice of morning, a spec in the sky,
Peeks through the keyhole of my child's mind.
Light catches my eye, first as a glimpse,
Past times seen as fresh as footprints.

Once more, I see those beloved faces,
Forming my life with familiar graces.
Ancestors seem to move through light,
To lay foundations in my life.

Relatives past seem alive; they are well,
Stepping through the veil saying, "pray, do tell",
Alive at home where they once dwelled,
They lived next door; we thrived so well.

My heart soft with love for Dad and Mother,
For making our home a cozy shelter,
Grandparents the keystones of our home,
Where light in windows, warmly shown.

A young child plays by the oak tree outback,
The breeze stirs the leaves; strong branches intact,
A call floats by on summer winds,
I hear the call, "Time to come in".

Transported back in a capsule of time,
I see through the window of my young mind,
Grandmother's face peers through the screen
Calling me in like a moonbeam.

I seem to be the young age of seven
As visions rain down on me from heaven,
Strong foundations built on love of—
        Beloved ancestors above.

Grandfather's Tool Shed

Breathing the smells of the damp, earthen floor,
While peering through cobwebs covering the door.
The tool shed is filled with sickles and such,
With old wooden handles, smooth to the touch.

The creaking of hinges; an old wooden door,
Summers of dankness rise up from the floor.
There in the corner a barrow waits, empty,
Removable sides for unloading its plenty.

Grandfather's treasures lined up on the sill;
Nails filling glass jars, threaten to spill.
A rake hanging down, a shovel or two,
A storehouse of measures surely will do.

I've not seen a place since nineteen fifty-five,
Where old tools were used always to survive!
Gardens were grown by the sweat of the brow,
With roosters and hens and a brown-eyed cow.

The tool shed sits empty; Grandfather long gone,
The shed has been empty for so very long!
Gone to God's heaven, the old man and his wife,
   Legends in time,
      Monuments to my life!

Grandmother's Kitchen

Grandmother's front door kept always unlocked,
Family and friends never needed to knock.
Not the ring of a bell or the slide of a key,
Always the home for sipping coffee or tea.

The kitchen alive with home-baked pies
In slices of apple and cherry surprise.
Folks gathered round for sharing old tales
Of far away places, never did fail.

Cupboards flung wide, an assortment of jars,
Fresh fruits and vegetables grown in the yard.
The stirring of pots, and the clatter of dishes,
The filling of tummies and small children's wishes.

The sound of a kettle, bubbling and hot,
The ticking and tock of a comforting clock.
Grandmother's kitchen, so full and alive,
For making fond memories—
     The home for our lives.

Grandmother Sings

I left her in the kitchen
Making wishes, happily,
Old songs, a true tradition,
When Grandmother sang sweetly.

Her heart was filled with love light,
Bonnie fair and bonnie blithe.
Songs sung with heart were cheerful
In her kitchen through the years.

And Grandmother sang,
"Don't sit under the apple tree
 With anyone else but me",
And, cheerfully, I agreed.

Grandmother's voice, soft and low,
And in my heart a rainbow.
A sweet lady and pleasant soul,
Grandmother will not grow old.

As she sings…
"Don't sit under the apple tree
 With anyone else but me",
Calling me to my memories
When grandmother sings sweetly.

Sharon E. Licht

Hi-Diddle, Hi-Daddle

Sunbeams and moonbeams, warm days in between,
The place where I'll go to encounter my dreams.
Back to the time of bright beaming sunshine,
A mid-summer's dream melts my heart, like ice cream.

Hi-diddle, hi-daddle; Hi-diddle, high-low,
Memories are sweet on a cradle swung low.
Stars in the night sky of ink hanging high,
White clouds whispering in morning float by.

A space in the middle between heaven and earth,
The home of my childhood and sweet memories' birth.
Hi-diddle, hi-daddle; Hi-diddle, high low,
I'll follow my young heart wherever I go.

19

Ice Skating Memories

Down on the pond frozen over with ice,
We'll put on our skates; circle around twice,
Carry ice skates; tie up the laces,
Wave to the neighbors with rosy red faces.

Winter has come; frosty air stings our noses,
Out on the pond in ice-skating poses,
Scarves bundled round our cheeks of red roses,
Last night the pond water froze!

Joyfully, Dad skates and makes figure eights,
As he slides his feet on the ice.
Dad spins me around, maybe once, maybe twice,
My Dad looks good on the ice.

I see Dad and me in my memory,
Skating with hearts young and carefree.
With love in my heart, clearly, I see
Dad following me, as he warmly agrees...

To carry my skates and tie up the laces,
And make figure eights, leaving his traces,
In winters alive with wind-kissed faces–
In winters gone by on the pond.

Lavender and Light

Dazzling is the twilight when fairies fly at night
Hiding in the trumpet vine of lavender and light.
Pretty leaves and berries laced with crimson red,
Climbing up the fence post out near papa's shed.

Enchanting is the moonlight where fairies dare to dwell,
Playing in the grapevine near grandpa's wishing well.
Four and twenty fairies twinkle round the vine
Of lavender and light, sheer gossamer entwined.

I watched a tiny fairy scale the garden wall
And perch atop the fieldstone; I prayed she wouldn't fall.
I watched small fairy shadows dance across the wall,
A symphony of wind chimes calling one and all.

Magic is the starlight when fairies swirl around,
Sprinkling the garden with dewdrops from the ground,
Polishing the berries with lace and crimson red,
Hiding in the lavender and light near papa's shed.

Magical Bugs

Where have all the fireflies gone?
Have children caught them, every one?
Their lights a delight for old and young,
Discovering them is summertime fun.

Blinking, winking, golden lights,
Flash like diamonds in velvet nights,
On again, off again, disappear!
Then, Mason jar captives reappear!

Fireflies flashing in star bright skies,
Dancing like fairies for searching eyes.
A child's pastime on a warm summer night
Is capturing the bugs of magical light.

Where have all the fireflies gone?
To the backyards of everyone,
Their mystical wings on a child's world,
A sheer delight for boys and girls.

Oh! Fireflies are truly magical bugs—
Like so many stars in a child's glass jug.

Memory Mountain

Big Chief Thunder Cloud,
Pretty Princess Summer Spring,
Painting pictures, drawing plans,
In their nowhere Badlands.

Round up all the horsies
Underneath the elm trees,
Little cowboy crony,
And that makes three.

Heading for the rocky pass
Up on Memory Mountain,
Trying not to belly laugh;
Ring around the fountain.

Pretty Princess Summer Spring,
Arrows made by bending sticks,
Tying them with tangled string
Around a bow is quite a trick!

Big Chief Thunder Cloud,
Folded arms across his chest,
Whooping loud, standing proud,
In his brave and boyish best.

Pretty Princess Summer Spring,
Ring around the fountain,
Weave a pretty flower ring
Up on Memory Mountain.

Molly

Oh! My golly! It's Molly!
My little chicken, a delight.
Oh! My golly! It's my hen Molly!
My Molly is a wonderful sight.

Oh! My golly! It's Molly!
I bought her when I was five,
Molly was my good hen,
Molly was my best friend,
The very best chicken alive.

Molly laid eggs every Sunday,
In her coop she laid them not,
To Uncle Jimmy's hound house,
Molly sneaked like a mouse
And chased those big dogs away!

Oh! My golly! It's Molly!
Her feathers were green and red,
She grew into a fat hen,
I turned to six then,
Molly let's always be friends….Until the end.

Oh! My golly! It's Molly!
My little chicken, a delight.
Oh! My golly! It's my hen Molly!
My Molly is a wonderful sight.

Mother Goose is Back

Mother Goose is back in her sunbonnet hat,
After fifty years through laughter and tears,
Mother Goose is back; now how about that?
Has she seen the queen in London, perhaps?

Come, run with Mother Goose down Drury Lane,
Laugh and sing through the sunshine and the rain.
Walk a crooked mile; wear a crooked smile,
Then, in Boy Blue's haystack, nap for awhile!

Like Mary's lamb, I've wandered distant lands.
I've found my way home; with rhyme I shall roam.
With my dearest friend from the land of pretend,
We'll buy a fat hen with the stroke of a pen!

And in the pumpkin patch under key and latch,
Peter's wife in pumpkin shell is doing well.
Come; play out back of the house built by Jack,
And find the mouse in Jack's sturdy stone house.

The ding dong bell means pussy's in the well,
Because little Tommy Tim put her in
By the whiskers of her little cat's chin.
The ding dong bell means kitty's in the well.

27

Mother Goose flew in on great swanlike wings,
With a soothing sound that makes my heart sing.
 Now, I can swing high in my blue-sky heaven,
The way I did when I was six or seven!

Mother Goose is back; bring the welcome mat!
We'll hang up her hat for a heartfelt chat
 Over English tea; now how about that?
Oh! Fabulous day! Mother Goose is back!

Mother Goose Memories

A strawberry day,
A far away time,
Barefoot through tall grass—
    Ponytails flying,
        Laughing.

Summertime slow,
Like cool lemonade,
A butterfly wind,
    A deep forest glade—
        Rustling.

Stone skipping frog ponds,
Sparkling, spring water,
Rippling rings
    Around fern fronds—
        Mirroring.

Cow jumping moons,
Jack 'n Jill pails,
Runaway spoons,
    Mother Goose tales—
        Sailing.

I cannot quite recall
The season or the day,
When my favorite Mother Goose took wing—
    And silently slipped away...

Old Sport

I remember the snores from Grandmother's porch floor,
Old Sport sprawled out near a squeaky screen door,
His long hound dog ears, all droopy and freckled,
A black and white coat, all shaggy and speckled.

I recall the sound of his hot, doggy breath,
Blowing like steam, furnace-warm and rain-wet!
 A nose, black like coal tunnels, so big and so round,
Wrapping dark nostrils around loud snoring sounds.

I remember forked teeth, the color of yellow,
Hanging hound lips, flapping, soft, like Jell-O,
Eyelids half closed on a doggy dreamland,
His paw print felt rough in the palm of my hand.

The pads on his feet, like pussy willows, but rougher,
Captain Hook toenails, yet, longer and tougher.
I remember the briars caught up by his fur,
Plucked out by small hands of the children we were.

Placing doll hats on the sleepy hound's head,
We covered, Old Sport, in a bright patchwork bed.
Dressing in doll's clothes, he didn't like much,
But he always put up with a little girl's touch.

Old Sport was a hunter; he'd seen brighter days
When running with rabbits on sunshine pathways.
My favorite old hound, tucked away in my memory,
His name in my heart; at home in posterity.

Remembering

A soft lullaby,
 A starlit sky,
Hush–a–bye,
 Time sliding by
 Rocking.
Berry picking,
 Grandfather clocks ticking
Barefoot toes,
 A garden hose,
 Family photos.
Roasting turkey,
 Coffee perking
Pumpkin pies,
 Children's eyes,
 Remembering…
Apple pies,
 Sunlit skies,
Crinkled French fries,
 Cherry surprise!
 Giggling.
Wiggling puppies,
 Fish and guppies,
Water bubbling,
 Nothing troubling,
 Meandering.

Big fat crayons,
Seems like eons,
Pastel looks,
Coloring books,
Drawing.
Clicking latches,
Coffee klatches,
Quilting patches,
Sewing sashes,
Mommies.
Yellow sunbeams,
Warm summer dreams,
Fresh winding streams,
Dusty moonbeams,
Sleeping.
A nursery rhyme,
Another time,
Yesterday,
Come what may,
Children.
Things I know,
Before I go,
A chimney stack,
A yard outback
Looking back.

Days of spring,
    A golden ring,
Baking string,
    Grandmother's wedding ring,
        Remembering…

Saddle Up

Saddle up the horses; time to take a ride
Over to the buttonwood, side-by-side.
In and out the windows of the trailing vine,
Over by the tangled woods where the fairies fly.

Saddle up the horses; time to turn about,
Watch the little elves play, short and stout,
In and out the windows chasing butterflies,
Over by the big woods where the fairies fly.

Time to see the ladybugs sitting on a branch,
Count the speckles on them if you get a chance.
Ride out to the meadow to the cottonwood,
Bring a fluffy blanket to sit on if we could.

Saddle up the horses, giddy up and ride,
Time to take a gallop where the fairies fly,
In and out the windows of the swinging vine
Trailing in the sleepy wood, run and hide.

Saddle up! Giddy up! Ride! Ride! Ride!
Time to hold your horses! Slide! Slide! Slide!
Running through the meadow where the fairies fly,
Maybe we would catch them if only we could fly!

Sweet Little Songs

Open the door to Grandma's house,
Oh! How the walls would sing,
As little hands reached to turn the knob,
Grandma's home was bright like spring.

Too-ra-loo-ra-loo-ra-lie,
Grandmother softly singing,
My favorite Irish lullaby
With distant church bells ringing.

Sweet little songs softly sung,
Her bright kitchen's melody,
My lilting heart enjoyed the fun
With "My Bonny Lies over the Sea".

When "Billy Boy" came home to sleep,
She sang, "Where have you been" tonight?
Those little songs will always keep
Sweet memories of sugar and spice.

Too-ra-loo-ra-loo-ra-lie,
Grandmother softly singing,
My favorite Irish lullaby
Like distant church bells ringing.

Teddy Bear Memories

I placed my memories in Teddy Bear's paws,
My childhood dreams, my wishes and all,
I shall cherish always those tender years,
And you, dear friend, through laughter and tears.

I recall the gaze of your black button eyes,
Your adorable face with eyes open wide.
My deepest secrets, I shared with you,
Old Bear, my friend, you've always been true.

You are the magic of bygone years,
You soothe my heart; you dry my tears.
My childish stories upon your ears,
Your cheeks so sweet, and forever dear.

I placed my cares in Teddy Bear's paws,
With frogs and toads with warts and all.
Old bear, you have been my steadfast friend,
From baby steps to the rainbow's end.

Looking upon your cute fuzzy face,
Carries me back to a state of grace,
Recalling times when life was a game,
In sunshine days when you chased the rain.

Sharon E. Licht

A Teddy Bear holds a young child's smiles,
And dreams of queens and long ago miles,
Tea cups and tea parties out on the lawn,
Golden Books, treasured; where we belong.

The Colors of Autumn

When I was a child, yard work was fun,
Raking rusty orange leaves through autumn,
Piling colors of yellow in high crunchy mounds,
As fluttering sounds made haste for the ground!

Pulling rake teeth through October's sparse lawn,
Unaware timeless hours would, one day, be gone,
Stacking leaf towers toward sun filtered skies,
Covering our bodies in autumn up to our eyes.

Hiding our giggles in the bunches we gathered,
Rolling with laughter until nothing else mattered.
Days filled with autumn, like dust in my nose,
Alive with bright colors when autumn's wind blows.

The Fruits of Summer

Come run with me through summer's newborn grass
When trees are full with cherries, ripe and red.
Come! Climb the boughs so full where fresh fruits bask
In shining sun hanging sky-high overhead!

Come, climb the trees alive with summertime's past,
Through rosy petals hung from leafy beds,
With summer's bounty held within a grasp,
The time for daydreams fills a child's head.

With baskets full, spread out 'neath cherry pink,
Enjoy the gifts of Mother Nature's hand.
On blankets, soft, relax awhile and think,
While savoring time lingering on pregnant land.

Come! Stay awhile and hear the lilting voice
Calling through windows wide with summer breeze.
For sunlight memories, let the heart rejoice!
The fruits of summer are eager to appease.

The Ornery Old Bard

There once was an elf in the yard,
He was an ornery old bard,
He went to the shed
For a piece of rum bread,
But the pastry went straight to his head!

When after the plump elf was fed,
I heard his nickname was Fred,
He recited his lines
Of old Maritimes,
And then went directly to bed!

Old Fred was an ornery old bard,
For years he lived in the yard,
He appeared now and then,
But I never knew when,
At midnight he often laughed hard.

There once was an elf in the yard,
He was an ornery old bard,
He had a grand time
Reciting his rhymes,
While keeping his teeth in a jar!

Sharon E. Licht

There once was an elf in the shed,

Singing and making rum bread,

But when I looked there,

The old shed was bare,

In a poof, he vanished, well-fed!

The Ride

I remember Daddy; it seems not so long ago,
He taught me to ride my bike; where did the gold years go?
I remember Daddy, alongside me, he ran along,
Running faster and faster saying, "Daughter, just hang on".

"Hold tightly to the handlebars, and soon you'll ride alone,"
"Daughter, you can do it!" "Don't be fearful." "Just hold on!"
My small feet peddled faster; the spokes turned round and round.
Dad held onto my bike and me and cheerfully ran along.

"Hold on!" "Hold on!" "You can do it!" "Just keep holding on!"
"I'm right here!" "You can do it!" "Daughter, you're not alone!"

I remember my Dad; it seems not so very long ago,
He taught me how to drive the car, so I would learn and know
That I could be proficient when one day I'd move away,
I should be self-sufficient, as Dad taught me yesterday.

"Hold on!" "Hold on!" "You can do it!" "Just keep holding on!"
"I'm right here!" "You can do it!" "Daughter, you're not alone!"

I remember Father as he walked me down the aisle,
Side-by-side, arm-in-arm, wearing a tender smile,
He said, "Daughter, you can do it." "This is your special day,"
With tears glistening in his eyes, he gave the bride away.

"Go on." "You can do it." "This is how life is meant to be,"
I remember dearest Dad, his love supporting me.
"Hold on!" "You can do it!" "I'm right here by your side,"
This has been my life with Father,
    And it's been a beautiful ride.

The Secret Hiding Place

Teddy bear's claim is not fortune or fame,
Teddy bear's treasure is a Hide n' Seek game.
Teddy bear secrets are, sometimes, overlooked,
Hiding in attics under ragged storybooks.

Old bear will you share your secret with me?
Step from the shadows and let my heart see
Button eyes gazing steadfast on old, golden dreams,
Tumbling from attics under old-fashioned beams.

Sweat bear! Can you hear through the marching of time?
Old bear, fast asleep under measures of rhyme.
Teddy bear will you step from your hiding place awhile?
And bring me the joy of an innocent child!

The Swinging Train

"All aboard; choo choo,"
"All aboard," shouts Lorraine,
 And we all climb aboard
    Our make-believe train.

Giggling, swaying side-to-side,
Faster, faster, our swinging train slides,
Swung from chains that click and clack,
    Lightening speed down made-up tracks.

Whistle stops made everywhere;
 Faster and faster from nowhere,
Down through valleys, climbing hills;
    "Slow down kids, before you spill!"

Thump, bump, bump, bump,
Thump, bump, bump, bump – all aboard!

"Where are you going," Grandma asked.
"Down to Texas, and we're going fast!"
Laughing, giggling, and holding on tight,
Passing ponies with delight,

Steer the engine; pull the caboose,
Shouting aloud, "we're sprung loose!"

"Stop that train," my Grandmother said,
"Before you fall and bump your head!"

Thump, bump, bump, bump,
Thump, bump, bump, bump – all aboard!

Chugging, slowly to a grinding halt;
Stopping in the station without a fault.
Remembering trains and swings recall
    A child's footprints on an old porch wall.

The Yellow Mixing Bowl

The big bowl is yellow; it stands in the middle,
The table so high, the young girl so little.
Standing on tiptoe, she dares to peek in,
The batter, all bubbly, is filled to the brim.

The hands on the bowl, like fingers on trees,
All gnarled and work-worn, flew like the breeze,
Whipping the batter in bubbles and twirls,
The beaters move quickly, the butter cake swirls.

The treat would be sweet in the June afternoon,
The girl having hopes of tasting the spoon.
The treat would be yummy, right down to the tummy,
Always delicious! A delight! Quite nutritious!

I am that small girl perched high on the chair,
Sampling the goodies grandmother made there.
This snapshot of time stands out in my mind,
As time takes its toll on the yellow ware bowl.

Grandmother's love and fond memories appear,
Baked goods in the kitchen soothing my fears,
The yellow ware bowl now sits on my shelf,
Filled up with memories, of Grandmother—myself.

There Goes My Heart

There goes my heart; here come my dreams
Wishing to walk along those bygone streams.
There goes my heart, flying back in time
To my childhood world of rainbows and rhymes.

I'll walk the ages on shores of old memories,
Running through the fields of pretty strawberries,
White feathered dreams in blue covered skies
With Sunday's child written in my eyes.

There goes my heart, walking down the line,
To a far away place in another time,
Running violet paths near buttercup streams,
Taking my little-girl time in blue-sky dreams.

Pitter-pat, my heart, I must remain true
To those golden days when things were new.
Something is to be said for those young-at-heart,
Keeping dreams alive, right from the start.

Crinkle-cheek memories, smiling happily at play
When I was a child back in yesterday.
Rosy-faced little girls in the neighborhood,
There lives my heart, in those days times were good.

There goes my heart, chasing big pumpkin dreams
In the patch of life held together, it seems,
By love and longing for tickling ivory days
When life turned around, like the sun in May.

There goes my heart, running to the sea,
To play in the waves; longing to be free,
Chasing after my dreams, footprints in the sand,
Catching fond memories in the palm of my hand.

Pitter-pat my heart, rat-a-tat my dreams,
Buttercup my world with strawberries and cream.

To the Moon

Flew to the moon in a beautiful balloon,
Chicka-chicka, chicka-chicka, chicka-chicka, boom.
Rocket to the moon in outer space; take first place in the space race,
Rock-a-sock-a, rock-a-sock-a, rock-a-sock-a, race.

Boosted up in time in nineteen sixty-nine,
High-a-fly-a, high-a-fly-a, high-a-fly-a, high!
To keep the American dream alive,
High-a-fly-a, high-a-fly-a, high-a-fly-a, high!

Put a man on the moon with a goggled face
Chicka-chocka, chicka-chocka, chica-chock-a, face!
Representing us all in the human race,
Chicka-chocka, chicka-chocka, chica-chock-a, race!

Then we walked on the moon with dust on our shoes,
Shick-a-shock-a, shick-a-shock-a, shick-a-shocka-a shoe.
And planted on the moon, the red, white and blue,
Flick-a-flag-a, flick-a-flag-a, flick-a-flag-a, flew!

Rode on the moon in a buggy for the dune,
Limpa-loba, limpa-loba, limpa-loba, Lune!
Then we sat on the moon with our bird's eye view,
Lune-a-moon-a, Lune-a-moon-a, Lune-a-moon-a, new!

We left the man in the moon our Stars and Stripes

Lune-a-moon-a, Lune-a-moon-a, Lune-a-moon-a-Flight!

Oh! "Say can you see" since our first lunar flight. Yikes!

Lune-a-moon-a, Lune-a-moon-a, Lune-a-moon-a-Sight!

We all had Dogs

When I was a child, we all had dogs,
We ran through our yards chasing frogs,
Taking for granted our one acre plots
Owned by families not by builders of lots.

Back in the day, some dogs had fleas,
Bringing fleas home to jump on our knees.
No big deal, we simply brushed the fleas off,
And washed down our dogs, drying them with cloths.

Back in the day, we all had front porch lamps,
Not a lighted patio the size of postage stamps.
Before the time of condominium dwellers,
We all lived in houses having dark cellars.

Back in the day, we ran outside freely,
Dogs needed no leads; there were no worries.
Back in the day, we chased crickets and frogs,
And we ran through the yards with a half dozen dogs!

And it seems to me, we all had dogs!

Back to Bucks County

Bucks County is a patchwork
Of small towns, arts, and crafts…

Back to Bucks County

Take me back to Bucks County
Beside the rolling Delaware,
On river views, I'm counting,
My heart belongs back there.

Walk me down a country road
Away from the beaten track,
To fragrant fields freshly mown
And farms of plump haystacks.

Walk along the dogwood path
To the Delaware canal,
Stroll along the towpath there
With white ducks and wild fowl.

Bucks County writes the pages,
Historical registries of the past,
Through wooded hills and sages,
My heart roams free at last.

Take me back to Bucks County
Where fields and streams abound,
Overflowing with nature's bounty,
And picture-perfect river towns.

Charm of the Farm

When years ago folks drove down country roads,
Bucks County's farms of charm laced countryside.
Like patchwork quilts, plowed fields spread far and wide,
While rows of corn were grown and oats were sown.

Fine dairy farms with Guernseys by the road
Delighted families stopping by the lane,
To watch tall silos filling up with grain,
To spot fat moo cows dotting country roads.

An education gleaned by fair carloads
Of picture-taking families on Sundays,
Stopping by farms to pass the time of day,
To spot the cows in pastures by the road.

Now half a century has come and gone,
And corporations bite the hands of time,
Devouring farmland, planting homes in lines,
Bucks County's farms are singing their swan song.

Bucks County's farms are shrinking over time,
With green space left to memories in our minds.

Come with Me to Bucks County

Come with me to Bucks County to roam the countryside,
Where waters swirl and tumble down Neshaminy at creek side,
The wandering pristine currents snake their way on by
    Rounding bends and ringing rocks,
        Where the daylight horses ride.

Slide down the hidden hillside near the Tyler family tract,
Where the Scofield wooden bridge sits knowingly looking back.
Over stream and meadow, time whistles through the cracks
    From the old bridge renovated,
        Preserving history's facts.

Stroll along the covered span; footfalls on wood-hewn planks,
Recall the old-time Wagoners crossing at tethered banks,
And American native people treading tender grounds—
    Shadows on the unbridled creek
        When morning mists flow down.

Come with me to Bucks County to a painted covered bridge
Grappling time and creek side beneath a rocky ridge.
Go with the flow of springtime and sunlight through Ash trees,
    And native fauna flourishing
        In a gathering early breeze.

Come with me to Bucks County
    Where time crawls from the past,
        Reaching out from bygone years
        Over creeks and bridle paths.

Life on Lenora

I lived on Lenora with Grandmother, Flora,
Dad, Mom and two Grandfathers, John.
Uncles, all three, Jim, Bill, and Ron
Playing games in the yard, out by the pond.

Cape cods and bungalows dotted our street,
Gravel and stones crunched under our feet.
Maple and oak trees swayed in straight lines,
Saluting S. Pennsylvania at the red stop sign.

No pavement or curbing stood in our way,
No gutters or drains, only short driveways.
Out in the yards, kids played by the dozens,
Laughing with friends and bunches of cousins.

Bicycles strewn out on the lawns of Lenore,
Chevys and Fords with black running boards.
Great Grandmother's house stood at the dead end,
And lawn mowers whirred loud, time and again.

Dads went to work carrying black metal lunch boxes,
Moms stayed home, gathering for town watches.
Clothes hung outside to dry in the breeze,
Townsfolk shared phones with lines called parties.

In summer front doors were flung open wide
For savoring the smell of food cooking inside.
Sugar in cups, loaned from neighbor-to-neighbor,
For baking a cake with that hometown flavor.

I'll always remember my sweet home on Lenora,
Dads drove to church in their Sunday fedoras.
Sweet buns at the bakery bought on the drive home,
A once-a-week treat when our sins were atoned.

My memories live on, down the Avenue of Lenora,
With Mom and Dad, and sweet Grandmother, Flora,
With Grandfathers, John; Uncles, Jim, Bill and Ron,
Out back in the yard, around the rippling fishpond.

Merry Christmas,
General Washington

Load up the tethered Durham boats,
Push off from the Delaware's shore,
Cross over to New Jersey
Before the Hessians storm the door!

Merry Christmas, General Washington,
The night grows dark and cold,
Time to defeat the enemy,
The battle must be bold.

The Durham boats cut through the ice
On the frozen Delaware,
The troops march on to Trenton,
Where victory will be declared.

Merry Christmas, General Washington,
We extend our heartfelt thanks,
As we re-enact your Christmas Crossing
Along the Delaware's frozen banks.

Morrisville's Main Street

I'll tell you a tale of a time long ago,
Back in the 50's and the main street I know,
Like the back of my hand, I remember so well,
This story is true: listen and I will tell.

Pennsylvania Avenue to Washington Street
On Bridge Street where hometown shoppers would meet.
First there was Pryor's, the pharmacy store,
With the soda fountain that's not there anymore.

Then there was Barber's a dress shop with hats,
Clothes lined the sides, hanging from racks.
Beaty at the counter, there across the back,
Near the cash register next to hat boxes that stacked.

For buying a watch, Reeso's was the place,
Johnny, the owner, knew everyone by face.
Sitting behind his new, glass jewelry case
With a small spyglass attached to his face.

The five and dime store, was just next-door,
Where footsteps squeaked on the old wooden floor.
The side counters were stocked up with toys,
And bouncy balls for good girls and boys.

Before going to the Cut Rate to have our lunch,
We'll go to the Morrisville Bank for a bunch
Of cash – in a stash – where it smells of Mahogany,
Where standing in line, forever, is like agony!

Let's drive down the street to the old Acme store,
At the corner of Bridge and Washington before Delmor.
We'll park in the lot on the store's other side,
And shop for groceries under the blue-purple sign.

Then up to Fooses' Market to purchase fresh meat,
A Mom and Pop store with canned goods stacked neat;
Fondly called "Foosies", because everyone knows,
The best chuck in town will be ground down for you.

I remember the Transit Diner, a bus-like affair,
Men from the mill would buy early breakfast there.
The waitress, I've seen in many movie films since then,
I know that I've seen her, but I can't remember when.

Just past the tavern there was Howell's old hardware,
For having keys made or buying treads for your stairs.
Herb and Nan Hooley lived in the apartment on top,
Next to Howell's Hardware, the regular old barber shop.

On down the street, now we're in the second block
Close to the bridge, a couple of vacant lots.
Cunningham's another hardware there that was brand new,
Until it moved uptown next to the fire house, Capitol View.

Morrisville's main street went by the name Bridge,
Alongside the Delaware over a Dyke's rock wall ridge,
You could see New Jersey and the capitol dome,
There, across the river, the monument shone.

The river carved a space between New Jersey and our hometown,
Separated by the Delaware as it churned, muddy down.
We could always count on the river water's flow,
And the stores on Bridge Street where we would go…

　　To shop for toys and other necessary things,
　　　　Where my heart grew its wings.

Ode to a Toad

Down in old Morrisville when I was a child,
Toads lived in the yard and made me smile.
Amphibious feet with tiny froggy toes,
Hopped around fishponds and Bucks County's roads.

I loved playing hop toad with these fat, little frogs
In summertime when they hid under dark logs.
When a fat-bellied frog hopped under bare feet,
Its cool, plump body made everyone screech! Eeek!

I recall holding a toad in the palm of my hand,
Its body felt cool; its toes felt scratchy, like sand.
The toad would wiggle a little if held too tight;
Yet, would sit quietly in a closed palm, if held just right.

Here's an ode to a toad and Bucks County roads,
And to the children who chased them
    Around their froggy abodes.

Remember the Mules (Of the Delaware Canal)

Preserve the canal, you say?
Clean up the towpath, you say?
Down in Bucks County, PA?
Remember the mules, you say?
From Bristol to Easton, PA?
On the Delaware Canal night and day?
On a sixty-mile, hand–dug waterway?

How was this dug, you ask?
A most tedious and backbreaking task!
With shovels and picks and axe,
Determination and mighty strong backs!
Built in the early 1800's, hey,
For transporting coal to market, you don't say!
Mules and barges on towpath and waterway
From Bristol to Easton, PA; a very long way, hey?

Remember the mules in elementary schools,
Teach our children barge mules are cool,
And the Canal is reserved for recreational parks,
Of the towpath and canal we are all a part.
Care for the canal and towpath, at last,
And enjoy bicycling along history's past.
Remember old families working with tools
On canal barges drawn by packs of mules.

The towpath and canal are Bucks County's jewels
And would not be possible without the mules,
So, what do you say?
        Remember the mules!

Running with the Hounds

We're off to the woods with our two eager hounds,
Following wagging tails and low bawling sounds,
Over the creek by a twig and stick bridge,
A beaver's dam built on a muddy ridge.

Cold noses to the ground, our hounds follow the scent
Of a muskrat trail; two sleuths, hell-bent.
Tripping through puddles on the leaf covered ground
Down in old Morrisville where the river runs down.

Dad and I were hunters on that cool October morn,
Along the winding trails of brambles and thorns.
Dad carried his shotgun over his shoulder,
And the autumn winds blew colder and colder.

I peered through a clearing in that swampy place,
Knee-deep in nature, face-to-face,
We followed the melodies of our two stealthy hounds,
Running down critters after low bawling sounds.

The Dogwood

I dream of the Dogwood, I dream of the snow,
I remember the dogwood from a long time ago.
Young branches covered in blossoms of white,
Like soft snow discovered on a mid summer's night.

These beautiful trees from a long time ago,
Soft, in my memory in the Bucks County I know.
Their branches reach out like unfettered rhyme,
Flowing like white clouds through the reaches of time.

Beautiful dogwood in the Five-Mile Woods,
Lovely flowers covering them as if they understood,
These Bucks County natives wear blossoms for show,
Gracefully growing at the edge of a meadow.

Are dogs in the dogwood out there roaming free
With puppies of plenty playing happily?
Their bark as silent as the mid summer wind,
Echoing through forests where the moonlight begins.

I remember the dogwood like new-fallen snow,
Blossoms scattered through spring from a long time ago.

The Patchwork of Bucks County

Bucks County is a patchwork of small-town arts and crafts,
The Delaware overflowing with inflatable rubber rafts.
A quilt sewn with bright colors of photographic green,
And woodlands full and lush; plush with evergreen.

Bucks County is a patchwork of historic stone farm homes
With dates of seventeen hundreds written on their stones.
A mix of different cultures blended with the land
Of folks who came before us with freedom in their hands.

German, Dutch, and English, and plain folk of the day,
A crisscross of cultures came to Penn's Purchase to stay,
Preserving farm and homestead with skeins of patchwork red,
And strong roots firmly planted inside the old homestead.

Bucks County is a patchwork and fabric of our lives
With antique clocks and furniture and homes with family ties.
A quilt of lovely colors made through centuries well laced
With every worthy vessel that landed in this place.

Bucks County is a patchwork embroidered with artists' flow
Through river towns and villages; wherefore the patchwork goes.

The Summer Fairies of Bucks County

The summer fairies rode currents of air,
By the hundreds dancing on sunlight fair,
Shining and shim'ring, they made their ascent,
Over tall grass, and fields, and streams, they went.

'Twas late in the morning one warm summer's day,
Between Wycombe and Furlong, a timely delay.
In lovely Bucks County; down a back road,
The fairies went sailing; on air, they rode.

This tale has been told by old folk and child;
How fairies were seen on a summer's day, mild,
When sunlight shines on the corn fields, just right,
One might observe this miraculous sight.

One day I traveled across a stone bridge,
Over the stream by the old bridle ridge,
I saw summer fairies dancing on air,
In lovely Bucks County in summertime fair.

Believe if you wish, now I've had my say,
I shall always remember that fine, summer day.

Towpath Travels

Quack! Quack! Time to look back
On the Delaware Canal,
Along its grassy, sloping banks,
    And walk the towpath trail.

Golden years have come and gone
When ducklings wagged their tails,
Immersed in murky waters
    On the Delaware Canal.

Quack! Quack! Take me back
Where orange webbed feet go paddling.
Quack! Quack! Splash! Splash!
    A dozen ducks go waddling.

Ducks delight in summers bright,
As along the canal I stood.
A happy sight in warm sunlight
    When Mother gathers her brood.

Fond memories are reflections
Looking back to bygone days,
Mirrors shining with perfection
    As ducks take to the waterway.

Away they go on the rippling flow
Paddling a watery trail,
Stealing the show as kids follow
    On the Delaware Canal.

Towpath treasures can be measured
By fond memories kept in tow,
Summer days and pastime pleasures
Of yesterday, this forever child knows.

CHRISTMASTIME

Christmas is a time for love
And wishes that you're dreaming of…

Christmas Pie

Remember cinnamon and sugar baked in a pie,
Memories of Christmas Past, the apple of every eye.
Pumpkin, spice, and sugar are comforting and nice,
Plum pudding, perhaps, will be shared at twilight.

A festive tablecloth by a lighted Christmas tree
Where trinkets sparkle, lavishly, for everyone to see.
A log thrown on the fire warms the winter air,
A cozy place to linger when family gathers there.

As Christmas Eve approaches, thoughts turn to home,
For gatherings with special folks, together, not alone.
The old house decorated with a wreath upon the door,
The patter of children's feet skipping across the floor.

Pop oversees the fireplace from his easy chair,
Knowing his loving family will soon arrive there.
Mom out in the kitchen prepares the evening dinner,
As Santa fills his sleigh on Christmas Eve this winter.

A glowing candle carefully placed upon the windowsill,
A welcome light beckoning; where stockings hung are filled.
A Christmas pie bakes slowly in an oven warmed just right,
For a festive family gathering on a lovely Christmas night.

What's in a Christmas pie if not thoughts of times gone by?
And memories of lighted homes and starry velvet skies,
Eyes twinkling by candlelight as friends and family greet,
And love for one another makes Christmas pie complete.

Christmas Tidings

Sleigh rides and caroling,
Bells that go ting-a-ling,
Old fashioned Christmases,
Traditional wishes.

Memories of Christmas Past,
Horse-drawn old carriages,
Post cards, Courier and Ives,
And Christmastimes gone by.

Sending a Christmas wish,
You're on my Christmas list,
Bright stars in diamond skies
As Christmastime draws nigh.

I remember Santa Clause,
Christmas Eves and puppy paws,
And what makes me happiest
Is togetherness on Christmas!

Sleigh rides and caroling,
Bells that go ting-a-ling,
White lights upon a string,
May Christmas tidings ring.

Christmastime

When Christmastime comes home to roost,
Stuff the turkey and cook the goose,
Place home baked cookies upon the tray,
To the merry jingle of Santa's sleigh.

Clean the chimney up to the roof;
Prepare for the sound of reindeer hooves.
A call and whistle, a bound and thistle,
Down chimneys cleared by brush and bristle.

When Christmastime comes home to nest,
Dress the table in Sunday's best,
Pour gladness in glasses, like sparkling wine,
And raise a toast to Christmastime.

Flying Reindeer

On an eve between Christmas and New Year's
When the air was frosty and cold,
It was then I saw three flying reindeer;
And I watched the magic unfold.

Whoosh! Up my street in a heartbeat,
As if they had wings on their feet.
And all I heard on that cold winter's eve
Was the sound of my pounding heartbeat.

There were only three I could see,
As I, quickly, ran down to the fence.
When the reindeer flew over the old garden bench,
They left not a trace of footprints.

I truly believe my eyes did not deceive
On that evening reindeer sprung before me.
In a flash, they appeared; in a wink, disappeared,
On the wind, they flew home, fast and free.

On an eve between Christmas and New Year's,
I saw the old man's flying reindeer,
As I stood on my porch in the cold, dusky dew,
In a breath, 'round the pine trees, they flew!

Glad Tidings

Christmas is a time for love
And wishes that you're dreaming of,
For hopes and dreams and memories,
For decorating the Christmas tree,
For hanging wreathes upon the door,
For baking cookies and shopping galore,
For wrapping presents with paper and bows,
For giving gifts to everyone we know,
For spreading good tidings, inviting friends in,
And gathering around fragrant evergreens trimmed.
A time for candlelight on windowsills
And stuffing stockings until they're filled;
Remembering a child, a wish to believe,
For goodwill to all, for glad tidings and peace.

Heart and Home

"Home is where the heart is," that's been said before,
And there's nothing like the holly on your own front door.
Home is where the candles glow on the windowsill,
And where a pot of coffee brews against the winter's chill.

You might find a welcome mat, or a cat or two
Curled up on the window's ledge, waiting there for you.
Or possibly a playful pup, a Pekinese, or Poodle,
Or, maybe a sleepy hound, or curly Labradoodle.

Home is your own castle, fit for queen or king,
Where all your dreams are possible; home is everything.
Home may display a flower box at the window's bay,
Filled with pine and evergreen for the Christmas holiday.

Yes, "home is where the heart is," it's been said before,
But there's nothing like the holly on your own front door.

Saint Nicholas

Remember old Saint Nicholas,
Bringing presents; giving gifts
To young children on his list,
His life story goes like this.

In the year 300 in the land of Turkey,
Nicholas was born in Patara, Lycia,
Later, he became a man with a plan
To give his gold to people of his land.

Saint Nicholas was a wealthy man,
Who gave away his fortune and took a stand.
Nicholas was a religious man,
His story carried from hand-to-hand.

Nick was imprisoned for his plan
And was later freed by the emperor man.
He continued to teach all over the land;
He took a stand and became grand.

Proclaimed a Saint for his good deeds,
And for all time everyone can see,
What his story means for posterity
With each present placed under the tree.

Saint Nicholas, Saint Nicholas,
We celebrate his life on December 6th
Hear his name and reminisce
About Saint Nicholas and Christmas.

The Ghost of Christmas Past

My eyes are filled like pools with salty sea,
When in my sight white Christmas lights do shine,
As evergreens with garland so entwine,
Melting my heart to pudding, instantly.

As through old crystal panes the lighted trees,
Do so consume my heart as to define
This unexpected view through windows fine,
With golden gifts of treasured memories.

Shadows of Christmas Past glide through gray mists,
Through early morning fog on old Newtown,
Before the keeper sees a soul around,
Ghosts arrive from seventeen seventy-six.

This flower shop alive in mirrored hues,
As through the Revolution, soldiers stood
Before this window; glowing tapers could
Light up the night for walks in history's shoes.

Back to the present, time through light does fly,
The ghost of Christmas Past caught by my eye.

Thoughts of Christmas Past

When in the comfort of my flannel thoughts,
Remembering all the Christmases I've known,
I see how fast my children, dear, have grown;
I count, like beads, the Christmas trees I've bought.

Watching the years like Stations of the Cross
With reverence for seeds of love once sown.
Like doves, aloft, these precious gifts have flown
To roost within the branches of my thoughts.

My loving children kneel before the pine,
How gloriously their wide eyes shine with joy,
Their expectations high with hopes for toys,
All wrapped inside bright gifts at Christmastime.

As sentiment wells in my aging eyes,
And memories of Christmas Eves flow by,
Portrayed as sacred pictures deep inside,
And in a flash, time shows how fast time flies.

As in a church my humbling thoughts take bow;
My life has reached its pinnacle, somehow.

FAMILY TIES

Treasures of heart and home
Shining on the family tree…

A Mother's Love

The feeling of new life fluttering inside,
On beautiful wings, Motherhood comes alive.
Nine months of a year preparing for birth,
Bodily changes measured in pounds and girth.
New life inside tucked away near my heart,
An infant triumphant is God's work of art.

One miraculous day, the birth process begins,
A warm cuddly bundle is the treasure within.
Mother's love grows with her new baby inside,
And there's nothing like a Mother's love and pride,
Mother's warm bundle placed in her arms,
To be cherished forever and kept safe from harm.

I remember the day you were placed in my arms,
I was your shelter; I kept you warm, and,
You are my God-given creation, my pride and my joy.
First, blest with a beautiful girl; then, a sweet baby boy,
These births are the true accomplishments of my life,
As a new Mother and a young woman and wife.

Today as my children are mature and grown,

Not far from my heart have they flown.

I'll love them forever; I'll love them for life

These gifts are God-given; they came from the light.

These are the souls God has entrusted to me,

To have and to hold for life and throughout eternity.

Child of Mine

I gave you life; offered you love and shelter from the cold;
You're in my heart; you're in my mind; you're in my soul.
Child of Mine, do you know you're my reason and my rhyme,
Can't you see you're with me all the time?

Remember the playground where I held your little hand?
We built those castles high and stood them rising in the sand.
Step-by-step and inch-by-inch you grew up big and tall,
Oh! Child of Mine, I'll be there to catch you if you fall.

Child of Mine, do you know you're my reason and my rhyme?
Can you see you're near me all the time?
Oh! Child of Mine, you've always been my lifetime light,
Child of Mine, your smile is my bright sunlight.

Can you see you're part of me, oh, my little one,
You've come into my life; you are my shining sun.
You're in my heart; you're in my soul; you're in my mind,
I'm letting go now; there's a mountain for you to climb.

You know I want to hold you and keep you from harm's way,
Your wide-eyed dreams are waiting on your doorway.
Go out and find your truth, your youth, your specialty,
Oh! Child of Mine, I love you so, can't you see?

Child of mine, do you know you're my reason and my rhyme,
Can you see you're near me all the time?
Oh! Child of Mine, you'll always be my lifetime light,
Sweet Child of Mine, your smile is my sunlight.

Dear Mother

As the years come and go
On the mercy winds of time,
In my heart, you're the only one
Who holds the tie that binds.

You are the perfect pastry maker,
Sweet seamstress who creates the clothes;
You are my favorite cookie baker,
And dear nurse who wipes my nose.

How very much I love you,
I only hope you know.
I could not ask for a better Mom,
And I love you for being you.

If I could take your hopes and dreams
And weave them into gold,
Like Rumpelstilskin, I'd spin away,
And give you the world to hold.

For My Daughter

My Daughter is a precious gift, a treasure most divine,
Brought to me on a special day in a blessed moment of time.
My Daughter was borne on angels' wings, from Cherubim sublime,
Now grown into a woman, a perfect pearl refined.
My Daughter's eyes, so beautiful with light pulled from the skies,
A perfect blend of lovely hues, Oh! How they hypnotize.
My daughter's laugh, intoxicating, it reaches into my soul,
Touching my heart with happiness, bringing me from the cold.
My daughter's smile, a work of art, sweeping me far away,
To distant memories of childhood, I cherish to this day.
My Daughter is my heartfelt dream, my birthday wish come true,
I pray she knows, wherever she goes, my love goes with her too.
As I walk the shores of life, I know I shall never walk alone,
For in my heart is a beautiful beach where seeds of love have blown,
Where a mother's love is nourished for a Daughter, who is now
    grown,
Where two lives are connected; where my dreams have flown.
There is nothing like a daughter; she comes from a part of you,
A precious treasure given to shine your whole life through.
I love my daughter deeply; I only hope she knows,
I will always love her deeply, wherever her footsteps go.

Friends and Family

If not for our relationships,
      We would be but empty shells—
So many pebbles on the beach,
      Drifting in tidal swells.
If not for friends and sharing,
      Sons and daughters one and all,
We would have no need for caring,
      Or for making our mark on the world.

Dear hearts give life meaning,
      For they show us we are not alone.
God gives us friends for leaning,
      As we wander on our own.
Friendships complete the circle
      And form the fabric of our lives,
Some stick like glue for a lifetime;
      Some fly in the blink of an eye.

Friends are similar to sea waves,
      Coming in and going out;
Friends share in our personal victories
      And our tears without a doubt.
The winds of our relationships
      Push us through rocky course,
And even through smooth sailing,
      Moves truth's underlying force.

Friendships act as mirrors,
      Reflecting our heart and soul,
A looking glass to our feelings,
      Sometimes stashed away like gold.
No matter the kind of connection,
      The style, the breadth, the length,
A treasure is gained as given,
      As friendships give us strength.

Life brings many blessings
      Bound by ribbons tried and true,
We cherish them as dear friends,
      Who are as meaningful as you.

Grand Daughter

A grand daughter is lovely, a beautiful light,
Grand daughter is golden; the light of your life.
She pulls down diamonds from starry night skies,
As seen by the twinkle in her sparkling eyes.

Nothing's quite as sweet as a little girl's hug,
All warm and cuddly like a bug in a rug.
As years come and go, as this little girl grows,
She is loved by grandmother wherever she goes.

Can you hear a sweet child chattering away?
To an imaginary friend brought to play?
An impish smile dimpling rosy-pink cheeks,
Can steal your heart any day of the week.

Dressed up in pink from her head to her toe,
As cute as a button, she is your rainbow.
She's sugar, she's spice; she's darling, so nice,
The joy in your heart makes a beautiful light.

Grand daughter brings light to a grandmother's world,
A treasure to cherish, a diamond, a pearl.

Grandson

There is nothing like a grandson,
An endearing little boy,
Some days he's rough and tumble;
Most days he'll make some noise.

He's Captain Hook on pirate ships,
"Walk the plank", imagine this!
He may be a super hero fan,
Of Batman, Spidey or Superman.

His toys strewn out across the floor,
Too busy to stop for daily chores.
Bath towel, his action adventure cape
When sharing his super hero's fate.

Caped crusaders, his avant garde,
His castle, a tree house in the backyard.
Thoughts of sports and baseball fame,
A wrestling match might be his game.

His interests lie in the world outside,
With frogs, and toads, and bugs that fly.
Barefoot in summers like Huck Finn,
Running footloose; time to come in.

He's full of life from morn 'til night,
A bedtime story; a kiss goodnight.
A grandson brings you starlight skies,
Each time you look in that little boy's eyes.

My Happiness

Once upon a starry sky,
I dreamed a dream of you.
Within that time, inside my mind,
In my dream, I knew you.

Once upon a summer's eve,
I watched the stars above.
Counting as they winked at me,
They spoke to me of love.

A noble place within my heart
Was carved and made anew,
A haven in the darkest dark
Where light radiates from you.

As a child, I always knew
One day I'd be right here,
Sharing with each one of you,
My joy, my love, my tears.

I always knew inside my heart
You'd bring me sunlit skies,
Happiness of the meadowlark,
Bright skies and butterflies.

Once upon a starry sky,
I dreamed a dream of you,
A gift bestowed in perfect time—
   My life and loving you.

My Son, My Shining Light

Through time and tide
And countless days, I've thought of you.
Even before your birth, somehow, then I knew you.
Your life held safe, protected warmly near my heart;
It was then I understood you and I would never part.

Within my fondest dream, I named you and called you Son,
Your life and mine entwined, as though we were one.
Your dreams became mine when your life had begun;
The tie that binds our spirits will never come undone.

As time slides by and as you travel life on your own,
The love I feel for you through time has warmly grown.
In depth and scope and being, in my heart I understand
Mother's love took form long before you became a man.

Son, the light that is your life shines like a distant star,
Leading my heart and mind to wherever you are.
Never far from home, or heart, or conscious thought,
Your life of quality so fine could surely not be bought.

With hues as bright and as true as gloriously golden suns,
As sure as the course to oceans flowing rivers run,
As certain as my love for you will never come undone,
My life transformed, made new, because you are my Son.

Although routines and schedules leave little time for talk,
I hope you know my love is near where your footsteps walk.
In thought, in mind, in spirit since you came into my life,
The little boy who became a man is, forever, my shining light.

Remembering Dad

I remember Dad, and the sway of his walk,
The sound of his voice; the gentleness of his talk.
His stature was slight; not big, but not small,
Dad was a plain man, not showy at all.

Here's to heart-to-heart talks out in the kitchen,
And the comforting feeling when I was with him.
He always had hugs, a kind word or two,
During talks over coffee, warm and fresh-brewed.

I remember Dad, and I miss him so much;
His calm, quiet ways, and his comforting touch.
Advice was forthcoming if only he was asked,
He seldom would scold or take me to task.

Dad was a kind man with tender, loving ways,
I will cherish his name to the end of my days.

The Bloodline Sisterhood

Our line of blood flows on year after year,
New generations thrive on ebb and flow,
The tie that binds our hearts, onward, we go,
Bound to each other's fate by blood and tears.

Climbing the steps of time along the way,
Heredity moves on the ties that bind,
A bond, unspoken, made in blood through time,
The feminine mystique must have its say.

Our fate is sealed forever in our time,
As each new baby girl comes to be born,
Our matriarchal sisterhood is formed
Within the line that is our blood's lifeline.

A masculine approach knows not our hearts,
Relinquished to the sidelines of our group.
The Sisterhood alone knows the plain truth,
That mothers, daughters, one will never part.

The Bloodline Sisterhood runs true, runs deep,
Connected by our hearts; those never sleep.

The Music of Mom

Here in the secret places of my heart,
There lives a spirit of gratitude and love,
A place where music plays eternally,
Connected to the soul who mothered me.

Here in this space plays a sweet refrain,
A gift passed on through Mother's able hands.
Sent here from heaven when angels blest her life,
And bore her down to earth on bands of light.

Here in this secret space my heart provides
A dwelling place where Mother's love survives,
Keeping safe her ways, her dreams, her life,
Since her days on earth as a Mother and wife.

Mom cherished family, those who went before,
Even after their spirits left through the door.
She kept their memory alive upon the wall,
In family photographs after their curtain call.

The memory of Mom has truly filled my soul
With music played to favorite songs of old.
Her music is alive inside my heart,
Like candles bright shining in the dark.

The Wonder Years

These are the years you will cherish the most,
Sunday mornings of scrambled eggs and burnt toast.
Magic moments with your children sprawled out on the floor,
These are the precious memories you will cherish and adore.

Days filled with sunlight and children's silly laughter,
Precious moments of today will last forever after.
Playtime all together on the living room rug,
And the little knees scraped when someone needs a hug.

The sweetness of your darling angels' innocent little faces
Asleep on their pillows after a day of bicycle races.
The sound of slamming doors, small footsteps through the house,
Ice cream stains on a freshly laundered shirt or blouse.

Baseball games, and field trips, dance lessons, and hockey sticks,
Plane rides and Disney World, popcorn and movie flicks,
And summers at the beach calling, calling, forever more,
These are the memories you will cherish and adore.

Today holds the wonder years your hearts will always know,
Warm forever moments as your beautiful children grow.
Blessed are the wonder years mirrored in memories—
Treasures of heart and home shining on the family tree.

Time and Tide

Bon jour, my daughters, time to walk with me,
To watch the sailing ships upon green sea,
To ride the waves on slowly shifting sands,
To gather glee from mermaids' ivory hands.

My daughters now it's time for sailing free,
As from our daily chores we gladly flee,
To write our song and sing sweet harmony
On winding shores to face our destiny.

Time to escape and shine our guiding lights
Through seaside mists and endless starry nights,
To offer up our laughter to the winds
And feel the salt and sun against our skin.

We'll send our dreams on wings into blue skies,
Releasing kites of joy to fly up high,
Then sing and dance to rocking melodies,
Together, strong, against the wind are we.

We'll find sweet love of life beside the sea,
Relaxing in our barefoot legacy,
In sea oats blowing free in southern winds,
With promises of love renewed again.

Let's place our footprints, firm, in ribbon sand,
Beside small seashells gleaned by searching hands,
Where time and tide, fair daughters, wait for thee,
Today, my daughters, let's go to the sea.

LIFE LINES

I love the twists and turns of life,
The serendipities that bring delight…

A Tribute to Life

I shall never be alone as long as I see a tree,
Growing high, majestically, a gift of life for me.
Alone, I shall not be when birds fly on the wing,
Stopping by to visit me, to feed, to drink, to sing.

When in the burst of morning, little creatures scamper by,
Like Saint Francis, I will greet them with love held in my eyes.
I shall never walk alone when God's orchestrated plan,
Repeats its solemn ritual upon earth's sacred land.

I shall never feel alone if my heartbeat stays in tune
With the sunrise of tomorrow, with every setting moon.
Keeping harmony with nature and every living thing,
I shall count my blessings, daily, as winter turns to spring.

Mother Nature's arms around me, viewing fresh dew-kissed grass,
And earth's flower-covered cushion to hold me to the task;
To sit, to pray, to listen to the heartbeat of today,
Accompanied by God's creations to white pines gentle sway.

Beautiful Light

Life is a light and a beautiful thing
Shining through seasons on summer and spring.
Outside your window, hear bluebirds sing,
High in the treetops before taking wing.

Sunlight and moonlight, the glow of the stars,
Beautifully shining on earth where we are,
Dazzling colors in silver and gold,
Such priceless treasures for eyes to behold!

Earth, alive in pure light is a beautiful thing,
Sun spun from shadows, tugs on my heartstrings.
Lovely is morning; my eyes are so blest,
A lifetime of sunshine brings true happiness.

Round beach ball moons shining out on the bay,
On dancing blue waves at the end of the day.
The moon sometimes borrows light from the sun,
A spectacular view when day is done.

The essence of life thrives in glorious light,
Sprung from the shadows both day and night,
Under cloud pillows in mantles of blue,
From embers of twilight, light shines through.

Today is the best day for being alive,
Glorious light touches pure hearts that thrive
On beautiful light of silver and gold—
    A spectacular view for eyes to behold.

Cheers to You
(A Wedding Song)

Cheers to the songs of love every written,
Cheers to the hearts that were ever given,
To holding hands and walking through dark times,
Long yesterdays through shadows unwind.

Three cheers to you, two lovers and dreamers,
Raise happiness streamers for wishes come true.
One sweet hello for lovers to lean on,
One star to dream on, three cheers to you.

Farewell to goodbyes, just greetings tomorrow,
Clouds passing by, sunlight over sorrow,
Two loving hearts, eyes filled with moonlight,
Sweet dreams in starlight, whispering tonight.

Three cheers to you, two lovers and dreamers,
Raise happiness streamers for wishes come true.
One sweet hello for lovers to lean on,
One star to dream on, three cheers to you.

Two hopes are renewed, two shoulders to lean on,
Two people to count on for a lifetime of love,
One great hurrah, a toast for the good times,
Togetherness lifetimes that dreams are made of.

Three cheers to you, two lovers and dreamers,
Raise happiness streamers for wishes come true.
One sweet hello for lovers to lean on,
One star to dream on, three cheers to you.

Home

Home is where the walls are warm,
Windows closed against the storm.
A pretty wreath upon the door
Welcomes you in, forevermore.

Home is where your daydreams stray—
In and out throughout the day.
Whenever you leave and go away,
Your heart sails home to end the day.

You may not be a queen or a king,
But home is a place to hang the key ring,
A space to hold your favorite things—
A familiar place tugging the heartstrings.

Home is a nest for settling in,
For pulling the blankets up to the chin,
To climb into bed and turn out the light,
A place of comfort against the night.

Home is a house brimming with life,
Sometimes shared by husband or wife.
Whether living together or living alone,
Home is where the heart loves to roam.

Life Lines

I love the sound a poem makes
When in fine lines its rhythm takes
Flight on wings of summertime winds
On mirrored lakes from deep within.
A Phantom flow purely refined
From sweet hearts, perfectly defined,
While born from dreams and reveries
Of ancient masters before me.
I dare to glimpse the masters' dreams
As words pour forth in silent streams,
Giving birth to summertime beams,
Of sun, and moon, and eyes that dream.
Poetry moves the swaying tree
Where to its bough a sparrow flees
To gently swing there, to and fro,
As so defined by divine flow.
Poetry tumbles from the tongue
When prayed aloud by someone;
As smooth as silk and satin gowns
Of southern ladies swirling 'round,
A soliloquy born of perfect blend
Embraces the poet like a friend.

Origins

Creation came and settled in my heart,
Like wings of doves aflutter deep within,
Bringing to light the places that were dark,
Where candles danced, flickering in the wind.
My heart took flight on dreams and reveries,
To nest among the sweet Magnolia trees,
Creating rhymes from distant memories,
A poem on a scroll was given me.
With ink and pen, carefully, I wrote the lines
As blown to me from off a distant shore;
A humble prayer created and defined
From pearls of wisdom He had placed in store.
Creation whispered in my inner ear,
And truth spoke to me gently, "I am here."

Silver String

A life is but a fragile thing
Suspended from a silver string,
Sailing along time's dusty winds,
    Life's metronome ticking within.

Life, the state of being alive,
A true desire to survive,
Learning the purpose of a life
    Gives flight to life to sail like a kite.

Like summer moths drawn to bright flames,
Love draws us in time and again,
Taking to heart brief specs of time
    When passions burn and spirits climb.

Over mountains, dangling from string,
As in that instant we've grown wings,
Life's purpose becomes crystal clear,
    To love when our soul mate draws near.

Should our loved one fly to the light,
We might fall in the dark of night,
Struggling with philosophies learned
And pain of loss as the heart yearns.

The years flow by like rivers, wide,
Before the mind can realize
How fragile is the string of life
And life can end; snap!
Day or night.

The Colors of Life

Life is neither black nor white,
    Always day or always night.
Life has rhythm, blend, and flow,
    And, after a storm, a rainbow.
I love the twists and turns of life,
    The serendipities that bring delight,
The déjà vu's and worn out shoes,
    Little surprises that chase the blues.
Life is filled with wonder and light,
    Sunshine gold and silver moonlight—
Nature's lantern to lead the way,
    Should we stray, night or day.
Nature paints with a visible brush
    In vibrant color to make the heart rush.
The canvas of earth filled in with blush,
    The time of the seasons; never a rush.
Life is not usually black or white,
    Rather, full of colors that bring delight
Blended by rhythm, balance, and flow,
    And a Master's hand that makes life glow.

The Curious Mind

The mind is quite a curious machine,
A plane that soars to distant, diamond stars,
And navigates a map to worlds afar
Then parks us in the corner of a dream.

Forgotten rivers filled from backward streams,
A secret passage holds old wounds and scars,
Then drops off to a door left slight ajar,
That hinges on a space long left unseen.

The mind is like a dredging rig offshore,
Which ties the line that tugs upon the soul,
And finds the chest which holds the pot of gold,
To make anew the view that went before.

The fisher casts his net off pictured shores,
And stashes cache in crafted, mindful holds,
Then blesses young and timeless tales untold,
While weaving truths that float the bobbing lures.

Like pirate ships moored out in shifting sand,
The mind floats on a long and lasting time,
That teeters on the brink where dreams began,
In oceans filled with deep and treasured rhyme.

The mind fueled by a universal force,
  With outreached hand,
    God holds our dreams on course.

The Legacy of My Love

The legacy of love moves on from age to age
In exhilarating moments of an exodus parade,
An innocent little heart beating next to mine,
Calling me through the doorway of my mind.

Infant triumphant! Fondly, I recall,
The beauty and the glory of it all.
Infant triumphant! A heavenly seed,
The legacy of my love is everything you need.

I remember springtime, your laughter on the wind,
Calling me to your side as the years rushed in,
With every heartbeat you will surely find,
Rose colored memories—inscriptions in my mind.

The ribbons of my love surround you every day,
Life's a celebration, dear, listen when I say,
"My love for you grows brighter with every dawn,
  With every night,
And with every multicolored candle that you light."

Creation is a priceless gift handed through eternity;
Passing on the torch of love, a mother's destiny.
The glory isn't over; it's just about to start
With a tiny infant snuggling heart-to-heart.

The Sketchbook

I am a sponge in the sketchbook of life
Absorbing sights and towering heights,
Like snowcapped mountains slopes of white,
Stunning in shimmering cloaks of ice.

My eyes like eagles upward fly,
Sailing winds in flawless skies,
Cutting through winds as a knife's blade,
Unveiling wonders God has made.

Some take for granted nature's prize
God has supplied for human eyes,
A perfect blend, the universe,
Nature's sketchbook, my favored verse.

The way the oak tree drops its fruit
Upon earth's soil for future use;
Acorns strewn upon God's good earth,
The mightiest tree must claim rebirth.

A timely schedule, earth spins 'round;
My feet stay planted on the ground.
The planet's pull of gravity
Is nature's law that lets me be.

I am a sponge absorbing it all
In nature's sketchbook from winter to fall,
A seamless blend from beginning to end,
The sketchbook of life, I must defend.

As a sponge, I soak it all in,
A wonderful world comes pouring in,
The expression of life; a miracle seen,
Like the life and time of a beautiful tree.

The Time of Dreams

Dreams have no schedule or table of time,
They rain down from heaven in the blink of an eye.
Scattered on soft winds, they fly with the muse,
Drifting on clouds, they delight and amuse.

Dreams are like fairies in a child's fantasy,
Lifting up shutters, wishing to be free.
Opening windows on a fresh summer breeze,
Dreams dance in the sunlight of old memories.

Dreams live a lifetime in the burst of a smile,
Having their vision in the soul of a child.
Dreams give to sad hearts a reason to fly,
They take flights of fancy in the light of an eye.

Dreams ride in style on a wing and a prayer,
Dressing in sunlight, divine comfort, and care.
Dreams gather teardrops from hurts of the past,
They sprinkle dewdrops on new morning grass.

Dreams travel the shores of our destiny,
Tearing down fences and walls to the sea.
Dreams drift with the waves of innocent tides,
Floating through time, dreams cannot be tied.

There's a Heartbeat

There's a heartbeat longing for the sunshine,
There's a sweet dream drifting through nighttime.
A ray of hope is peeking through the clouds at you,
Make a wish; believe your dream will come true.

There's a white cloud floating in a dark sky,
There's an angel flying there on high.
There's a blue-sky canopy above you,
Time to find your spectacular rainbow.

There is a hunger crying to be fed,
There's a poor man wishing for a soft bed,
There's a world longing for sweet harmony,
Oh! Bless the light and grant us liberty.

When your heart is longing for the sunshine,
Make a wish for your dreams to come true.
Find the bright cloud in a summer sky of blue,
Just believe and your dreams will come to you.

There's a heartbeat longing for the sunshine,
There is a sweet dream drifting through nighttime.
A ray of hope is peeking through the clouds at you,
Make a wish; believe your dream will come true.

Turning Seasons

Pine trees shed their needles on a carpet soft below,
And the sleepy morning sheds its light with an eerie orange glow.
The fall winds keep on churning, temperate from the south,
Iscariot winds kiss my cheek; they turn my life about.

Daybreak rises mild, a banana boating wind,
While tropic air feels naked brushing against my skin.
November has a greedy hand, stripping tree branches bare,
Pulling back the temperature from chilly winds to fair.

Wearing many faces, seasons change from day-to-day,
Like a turncoat trading places, holding winter winds at bay.
With the season slowly turning and its offering of lovely days,
Thoughts turn to love and yearning; those were lost along the way.

In the space of nine and eleven lurks the changing of the guard,
While on the other side of heaven, someone plays the joker card.

PATHWAYS

Today I shall walk the secret path
I must journey there alone…

A Beautiful Soul

You're a beautiful soul
Born from lost days of old,
Dreaming of blue skies
    And angels' bright eyes.

Through the meadows of springtime,
Baptized by rain,
You followed the sweet sounds
    Of your angel's refrain...

Cherubim and Seraphim
Have sung songs for you
In the halls of great mansions,
    Where your spirit once flew.

Your hair flecked with golden,
You traveled your path
Along highways and byways,
    Where young children laughed.

Don't ever weary
Or tire of life's song,
Let your guardian angel
    Carry you along,

Because you are golden,
You have been truly blest,
Through lifelines and bell chimes
    With sweet happiness.

You're a beautiful soul,
You've flown with the winds,
Blown straight from heaven
    At the time you came in.

Others are drawn to
The style of your smile,
Your unique ways,
    And your love of yesterdays.

Counting the blessings
Only you could bring in,
I'm pleased to know you
    And call you my friend.

A Familiar Face

How lovely, this place with familiar face
With stepping stones carving a secret place,
Fat, juicy plums plopping straight down—
An assortment of purple flattering the ground.

Embracing my heart, the garden in bloom,
A beautiful space kissed by sunshine and moon.
Its power in blossoms and swaggering vines,
Pulling me back to a fleeting moment in time.

Bell-skirted ladies in sunbonnets, sow,
Sweet William and Foxglove happily grow.
Daisies in yellow; vines trumpeting in pink,
A trail of red roses over a curved arbor's brink.

A white picket fence holds back vines gone astray,
To keep them from running away with the day.
Flowers, like children, need space to roam
And safe harbors for climbing or playing alone.

With showers, flowers grow lovelier each day,
Brightly waving along their merry cockleshell way.
With a strangely familiar and ladylike face,
The garden whispers from a world of fine lace.

All for the Beat of Your Heart

Take a moment in time to find a new meaning,
Your life is alive and blessings are streaming,
Through your heart, through your mind,
Sunlight is streaming, all for the beat of your heart.

Rise from your sleep, and peek from your window,
A new day to keep rises before you;
And your love is alive walking from shadow,
    All for the beat of your heart.

The memories are there, fresh from the old days,
Each day was the same, routines as always,
You weep for the past, but old days cannot last,
    All for the beat of your heart.

Walk on, look ahead, you'll find your rainbow,
After the storm when you peek from your window,
And your life is made new, without further adieu,
    All for the beat of your heart.

Open your eyes; a new day is before you,
Don't be surprised; the sun shines for you,
Delight in your dream like peaches and cream,
    All for the beat of your heart.

Here is the clincher; you are the winner,

Summertime has arrived; your star shines inside,

Your spirit was spent; yet, now is content,

    All for the beat of your heart.

Call Me Columbus

Today, I might sail as Columbus did
To find a bright new world,
Discover the end of the rainbow's bend,
And gold, rubies or pearls.

My journey might be over tranquil seas,
Where daylight comes and goes,
Or a monster might creep beneath the deep
Dark Ocean's unknown flow.

Yet, I must set out on this date and time
And sail out to the brink,
Discovering the treasures that lie ahead,
And pray my ship won't sink.

To satiate my hunger, I'll cast my line
Into the ocean's swell,
Patiently wait for a nibble or bite,
Hoping my line will tell.

Today, I'll set out as Columbus did
And sail out to the deep,
My eyes on the prize of discovery,
On seas where mermaids sleep.

Like Columbus, I shall hoist up my sails,
I'll head into the wind,
Fly over the sea where I will fly free,
Where my daily log begins.

Call me Columbus, the explorer kind,
With dreams of ocean time.
I'll sail the tide to the end of the line,
And bask and thrill in the find.

Crayon Colors

In the moving meadow in sunshine and light,
My eyes soak in a beautiful sight,
Lively crayon colors flow into a spread,
As if a quilt is designed for a royal bed.

Exquisite gold leaf streams down the slope
And over the ridge in reams of pure hope,
As drawn by an artist's invisible hand
In breath-taking rainbows over the land.

Passionate purples stake out their claim
Crisscrossing the valley and carpeted plain,
Delicately trimmed in babies breath lace,
Entwined by sunshine's newborn embrace.

Scarlet ribbons flow, gracefully, up a hill,
Encircling the place of the whippoorwill.
God's paint pail seems to have tipped and spilled,
And through the meadow His colors filled.

God's canvas spread out in a rainbow array,
While assortments of colors swing and sway,
A gift for my camera's picture-perfect eye,
In a split-second beneath a cotton cloud sky.

A glorious page of national geography
Portrays this moment in mind's eye photography,
As crayon colors stream over the field—
    In lovely purples, pinks, red, yellows and teal.

Formality

There is a place for formality,
A time for grace and normality,
An expression of purpose in meter and rhyme
In the structure and form of a poetry line.

The truth of expressing formality's form
Is written in lines where structure is born,
Giving heart meaning to the dim world within,
As seen by the poet who searches therein.

The world seems opposed to beauty and grace,
Where evil runs rampant in time and place,
Trying to capture the whole world's attention
With the starkness of civilized, modern convention.

Formality finds its beauty and purpose
Circumventing the world and earth's daily circus,
Rising above wars and arid desert winds,
By finding pure meaning and truth within.

Give me formality in trying times,
An expression of truth in a poetry line.
Structure and form give birth to a rhyme
And beauty for all seasons in a poet's curved line.

Good Day Sweet Muse

Sweet and silent syllables
Tumble from my pen,
Another day is on its way,
    And we're writing once again.

Good day, sweet muse, today we meet
 To trip the primrose path,
 To skip along on feathery feet,
    To hear the sunflowers laugh.

You chose me for your student,
You taught me very well,
Giving literary movement
    To words for show and tell.

I dare not take the honor,
For the honor is shared by two.
Sailing in on sparkling waters,
    You appeared right out of the blue.

The artist's flow has spoken,
As you hone and perfect my craft,
Our bond cannot be broken
    When you take me to the task.

Fly me away to the meadow
With its bright sunbeams at play,
Dancing like children's shadows
    On a perfect sunlit day.

We shall visit Christopher Robin,
Share a spot of honey with Pooh,
Or sneak a peek at a Hobbit
    Walking in pointed shoes.

We shall leave behind the old world
 And civilized pursuits,
At heart we are as young girls
    Putting our dreams to good use.

Good day again, my dear friend,
I shall take a moment or two,
And discover the end of the rainbow's bend
    And happily walk in your shoes.

Inca Blue

Without a world of dreams within,
There would be no earthly reason
For hearts to beat time and again,
As the earth moves through four seasons.

Within the world of inner dreams
Lives a genie in a bottle,
To be released like clouds of steam,
To a world spinning full-throttle.

To spring from out her crystal tent
With sweet dreams and wishes come true,
Of golden seashells to be spent,
Underneath skies of baby blue.

The seeds of youth have long been placed
In her bottle of Inca blue,
Charting times when innocence graced,
A child that rhymed in play shoes.

Within my soul, I see the world
And small wonders of the ages,
Page after page to be unfurled
By the genie of wise sages.

I'll not come out empty-handed
From the place of deep Inca blue,
Where genie has taken my dreams,
Granting these words I write for you.

My Fortunate Day

I'll find my fortune hiding under early sunlight beams
In a wooded forest glade near a rushing old millstream.
I'll watch for wood nymphs tiptoeing timidly through the trees,
While tiny fairies brush their wings against a silken breeze.

When the forest first awakens and rubs its sleepy eyes,
And the last moonbeam has faded under shadow and light skies,
I'll listen for the songbird singing notes in trembling trills,
Signaling daybreak's symphony soon heard on yonder hill.

My fortune shall be found veiled in early morning's light,
When God's creatures first arise from their cradle of the night,
And a furry squirrel or rabbit scamper by my searching eyes,
Before running through the dappled day under cosmos skies.

With joy, I shall awaken on this fortunate dawning morn;
Seek out the witty weaver spinning webs in pattern form.
It may be that I will see her before going her leggy way
To hide inside a hollow log on this, my fortunate day!

My Solitary Dream

Love, life, and truth glide inside my dream,
Riding my psyche on God's golden stream,
Sailing on words saturating my brain,
Mumbling, tumbling like existential rain.
Formed in rivers ordained to flow free--
Structure and meaning destined to be.
Something divine runs up and down my spine
Stimulating synapses; syntax defined.
Synopses give rise to my sublime work
Created on the day sunlight gives birth.
Dazzling, sparkling, oceans of light,
Kiss the shores of my soul, a solitary delight.
This dreamer's gold on a transcendent beach
Shines transparent, like sea glass within reach.
From the depths of my dream, soliloquies waiting
To be baptized at this dreamer's awaking,
When the hush of the rain falls endlessly
On a blank page in a white paper sea.

Sweet Solace

Along the pathways of my wandering mind,
Where years gone by take shape and form my life,
A gentle ghost walks in and calms my night,
Sweet solace floats the dream on temperate climes.

How difficult to leave such space and time,
Lost in this moment held up to daylight,
Its truth, a featherbed that feels just right,
A dear old friend once lost, once left behind.

My robot self performs the rites of day;
Yet, in my heart I'm called to rambling streams,
Those wander from my past like bright sunbeams
Requesting but a moment's gentle sway.

Sweet solace brings the sunlight to my thoughts
And disregards the leash of time that pulls,
Withstanding segments of my life now full,
One eye on time, sweet solace climbs aloft.

While blowing through my soul like windswept sand,
Sweet solace takes its leave from time's command.

Sometimes It Rains

Listen to the patter of the early morning rain,
Falling soft and gently against the living plain.
I turn around and listen as someone calls my name,
Saying, "Life is as it should be and sometimes it rains."

In the misty morning when the rain falls softly down,
And living things are hiding under soothing tapping sounds,
I'll be here in the solace of my seasoned memories
Of sailing ships on blue waves across the deep green sea.

Allow the laws of nature to create our hopes and dreams,
The way stars form the Milky Way in brilliant winding streams.
Memories of rippling waves brush the winding virgin shore,
Leaving treasured gems of purpose not to be ignored.

I'll round up my memories, wild horses on the plains,
As I sit here and listen to the patter of the rain,
And draw upon the pictures in the sketchbook of my mind,
Knowing life has meaning and all beings have their time.

Hear the pitter-patter of the gentle drops of rain
I question, who is going there? Who is calling my name?
A reply is heard like angels' sighs, "It's your destiny",
A clandestine meeting with the angel guiding me.

Held within life's purpose and my arriving destiny,
I'll serve my time on earth, knowing what is best for me,
And write down my remembrance of everything I see,
Depending on the hand of God to solve life's mysteries.

All things have their purpose; time to sing life's sweet refrain,
Today as destiny has told me, sometimes it rains.

Somewhere in Time

A picture-perfect sunshine day,
Where breezes flow and sparrows play,
A secret garden swings and sways,
Somewhere in time; somewhere today.

A Robin's note on stirring winds,
This lovely sun drenched day begins,
Sweetness drifts through small hometowns,
While gold-brushed ribbons touch the ground.

Somewhere in time; somewhere today
Hear children's laughter while at play,
Pattering feet with rhythm and beat,
And footprints made by little bare feet.

Somewhere today; somewhere in time,
Old blankets lay in gold sunshine,
Small shoes left on green apple lawns,
Forgotten, when summer sings her song.

Sunlight scenes splash through my mind,
Somewhere today; somewhere in time.
I'll catch sunbeams along my way,
Somewhere in time; nowhere today.

The Promise of Morning

Come gently to me, morning, bless my awaking heart
With music of the living in this flower dappled park.
Bless me with your sunlight held in golden beams,
Touch my heart with memories of timeless, treasured dreams.

Speak kindly to me, morning; my heart is on the mend,
Reaching out for solace from a world so cruel, again.
Wrap me in your blanket of sunlight shining 'round,
Embrace me with your chatter of cheerful sunrise sounds.

Sing softly to me, morning, on your fresh, fulfilling breeze,
My heart belongs to sunlight, soft breezes through the trees;
And the trickle of gentle raindrops pattering on the pane
To wash away my sorrow with drops of intermittent rain.

It matters not if morning brings gold sunshine or rain;
But, the assurance of renewal on this mundane earthly plane.
I count on morning's glory to bless my life secure,
When promise of her beauty arrives at my awaiting door.

The Secret Path

Today, I shall walk the secret path,
I must journey there alone,
To hear the sun and moonlight laugh—
The place where sins are atoned.

Sitting down with myself and God,
Where dreams melt away the stone,
A visionary life clears away the fog
On the pathway traversed alone.

Like birth and death and sacrifice,
And raw truth that storms the soul,
An earthbound life must pay the price
For a God-given key to hold.

From golden phrases, daily drink,
And a note is superimposed,
Making an everlasting link
To compose what the heart knows.

Once more, today I must travel there,
Taking pen and ink in hand,
Producing a score so fresh, so fair,
Created by the Master's plan.

Along the path that is traveled less,
Between the spaces of my thoughts,
I shall find the poet's warm caress,
And truth blest in a book of cloth.

The Scribe

I am a scribe who writes before the King;
I write the truth and loves creates its wings,
I am a soul blown free from eons past,
Traversing seas of centuries; love, my mast.

I know the truth that moved through Moses' hands,
When he received the laws laid on his lands.
I hold the Holy Spirit in my grasp;
I paint the hieroglyphs golden asp.

I am a soul, who's seen the years of old,
A moving energy that will not fold.
As long as I receive these truths from thee,
I shall remain a slave who's been set free.

Every word I write is from eternity
Where God has given truth His energy,
He came into this world to make a light,
To bless the time we have to make it right.

I am an energy most like the wind,
My thoughts have flown to heaven and back again.
As David wrote the psalms, I write for thee,
And wisdom of the ages writes for me.

I am a scribe within the kingdom's walls,
I walk among the angels' ivory halls,
With legions of archangels guiding me,
Along the living sea in Galilee.

There is one truth that every heart must know,
The force of God creates the artist's flow,
And moves the pen creating written words,
Passing over men before being heard.

I am a scribe within the temple's walls;
I write on scrolls kept safe in sacred halls.
This is my heart and soul; this is my call,
To scribe the hearts on earth before the fall.

I am a scribe, who has been blest to write,
This scribe's inscription on this very night.

The Writing Cave

I'll crawl inside my writing cave
Where the poet's eye can see
A dancing fire that leaps and waves
To the Shaman calling me.

I'll look into his wise old eyes,
I'll search his knowing smile,
Then seek the ever-present prize—
A script in scrawling style.

I know not what mysteries sleep
'Neath a canopy gray with years;
Nor which tales he'll choose to keep
Or bless, when the talisman appears.

Might the wheel of life gone by
Turn the ghosts inside its spokes,
And show the haunts they must fly,
Through ribcages of present folk?

Wide awake in a hypnotic state,
In a small cave's scrawling room,
I stretch my arms to the hand of fate
And the Shaman writing in the gloom.

Walking on Clouds

This is your gift falling from heaven,
As soft as white snow, words freely given,
To be used with wisdom wherever you go—
Footprints through time, over the rainbow.

With dreams lifted up on a whispering wind
And heart warming feelings deep from within,
On torrents of words rising and falling,
A still voice keeps calling; asking to come in.

A poet walks softly on the wings of the wind,
With a gentle heartbeat stirring within.
There is no drummer or loud beating sound,
Only a lovely white dove where peace filters down.

A poet walks quietly with head high in a cloud
Searching for truth not yet seen by the crowd,
To write, to compose, to seek throughout time,
To create from heaven, a rhythm defined.

With the tool of language and the stroke of a pen,
The poet writes the truth again and again,
A gift of purpose while courting the muse,
Walking on clouds with white wings for shoes.

Recalling the past in a blink of an eye,
Memories flow light in a bright rainbow sky,
Charging the future in a small crystal clearing,
Lighting dark corners with sweet words, endearing.

Never measuring one's life with another man's rule,
Rather, opening closed doors with a sharp writing tool,
Entering with harmony, holding heaven's still hand,
The throne room to search with fine language command.

Walking on faith by a light empowering force,
And the will of the heart to follow its course,
A poet, an old friend, rides out from the past,
Delivering a promise as bright visions enmasse.

A quiet knowing settles down on the soul,
As a gentle reminder to come in from the cold,
From a world stark with falsehoods and meaningless chatter,
To create the heart's meaning where nothing else matters.

The truth of expressing deep feelings within
Will open the present that God has dropped in.
Walking the thin line between things real and unseen,
Shines sunlight renewed through the gray mist of dreams.

Where lies the purpose of the gift of the soul,
If not to bring joy to hearts left out in the cold?
A promise of solace to a world wracked with pain,
And life made anew from old memories slain.

Up and away, a familiar poet is dreaming today
Of building light bridges in a small, knowing way,
To regain the balance on a line thick or thin,
To enter the King's chamber held sacred within.

Rise up dark world on a wing and a prayer,
To horizons of sunbeams waiting to tear
Through the fabric of life stuck in twilight,
Creating for you, a new heartfelt delight.

Moving through mists of memories and dreams,
A poet magnifies life like a speck on a stream,
Floating through morning on a gift of white wings,
Rising on clouds, illuminating everyday things.

Come into my world and open your eyes,
And make room for visions through a poet's eyes.
Days rise and fall like a serendipitous surprise,
Dreams; reflected anew in glowing gold skies.

If I had my way, the world would be filled with books
Containing only blue skies and tumbling brooks,
Where beauty pours forth from the words held within,
Going back to the first day where creation begins.

Walking on clouds is easy, it seems,
When a heart is willing to follow its dreams.

SEASCAPES

My favorite place to be
Is by the sea...

A Sea Island Day

Down on the shores of clear, crystal, sands,
Beside the blue ocean, a glorious strand,
A pearl of perfection, a spectacular day,
Sunshine designs a perfect beach stay.

The taste of salt air on welcoming winds,
The feel of warm sunshine on winter white skin,
A sea island day beside slow, shifting shoals
Clears out the mind and nourishes the soul.

Carolina designs summertime, so fine,
Pulling me in like a fish on a line.
Peach colored sunsets and big beach ball moons,
Play on my heartstrings, a beautiful tune.

Oh! Sail me away on a sea island day,
To kick back and relax, to let come what may…
There's a warm southern wind stirring today,
Dancing through blue on this perfect sea island day.

A Seashore House Blessing

God bless this house beside the sea,
Keep it safe indefinitely.
Make its floors, windows, and doors
Strong against sea winds and storms.
May everyone who enters here
Find happiness and good cheer.
May all find shelter from the storm,
Settle back and feel reborn.
May comfort dwell within its walls,
Here in this lovely port-of-call.
May laughter ring from deck and rail,
May sunny days never fail.
May all good friends and family
Find safe haven beside the sea.

A Wayward Soul

I'm in slow motion and my heart's not here;
I'm by the ocean with beach blanket near.
Palmettos wave and dance with gentle sway,
Beside the seashore dressed in silvery spray.

Blue Ocean's motion is a soothing sound,
Along warm southern shores, I'll lay me down,
And travel on the kind, caressing winds,
Those call to me through time where tides begin.

I am a wayward soul most like the wind;
I travel pathways splashed from dreams within,
As ghostly sailing ships traverse the seas,
So do old dreams of oceans carry me.

I hear the mermaids from the deepest sea,
So softly calling to the heart of me.
Their sounds forlorn; yet, sweet upon my ears,
Remembering other times and distant years.

I'm in slow motion, wayward, I'm not here,
Beside the ocean, listen; do you hear?

Anchors Away

Sails and snails and dolphin's tails,
Wandering where the sea moss trails.
A sleepy lagoon by sun and moon,
The air's in bloom by May or June.

Sails and pails, a seaworthy tale,
A small house waits with deck and rail,
Watching where the shrimp boats sail—
A port from storm and tempest gale.

Sails and pails, a wandering wave,
Rolling away where dolphins play,
Pull up the anchor and take me away
To bide my time awhile and stay.

Sails and pails and sand digging spoons,
Scattered on sands where seagulls croon.
Take me away to a backyard bay,
Where I'll hideaway; anchors away!

By the Sea

Ocean breeze,
    Florida Keys,
Sandy toes,
    Tidal flows.

Shifting sands,
    Mermaids' hands,
Sailboat sails,
    Dolphin tales.

Rolling oceans,
    Suntan lotions,
Palm trees sway,
    A moonlight bay.

Orange beach ball sun,
    Day is done,
Tidal pools,
    Fish in schools.

Bathing suits,
    Footloose,
Fancy free,
    By the sea…

Catch the Sea

I'll catch white sea foam in my hands,
Stirred up by surf and churning sands.
Sea suds fly out on laundered winds,
While silken sea mist soaks my skin.

I'll catch the breeze this sea filled day,
Like a sea nymph at child's play;
Then, smile and pose for my picture book,
And catch the sea by hook or crook.

I'll scoop up sea foam with bare hands,
Then race the sun on wind-swept sands.
I'll catch clean sea in small degrees,
Beside the sea, the catch is free.

Free By the Sea

We danced on the sand, flashlights in-hand,
When the night was ink at ocean's brink.
We howled at the moon late night in June,
Down by the sea, our energies sailed free.

Three vessels of mirth beside thundering surf,
Staggering with glee beside the deep sea.
Sea winds flung our sounds back in our faces,
As we moved to the dance of destiny's paces.

We left our marks on sandy hill places,
That night when the sea wind was faceless.
Three women defied age, gravity, and time,
Our energies flowed free like sparkling wine.

Majestic sea ladies on wandering shorelines,
Played witness that night in North Caroline,
Joy overcame us; laughter our sign,
Borne on the winds of sea, space, and time.

To dark winds and skies, we danced in the sand,
We sang heart-to-heart; woman to woman.
Hopelessly free were we by the sea—
Invincible, in the hands of eternity.

That night in my mind, a beacon through time,
On the great dunes designed by Caroline—Ah!

Island Paradise

Down by the ocean under sun and sky,
There is an island kissed by gentle tides,
Surrounded by salt marsh and tidal pools,
Where seashore creatures thrive; nature's jewels.

There is a strand of sand by sound and sea,
An island paradise that waits for me,
With tiny seashells washed up on the sand,
Small treasures to be found by idle hands.

There is no hurried place in such a place,
But time to feel warm sunshine on my face,
While finding hidden pathways to the shore
With easy southern living underscored.

A place where gentle seasons come and go
Is where I'll go to feel sea breezes blow,
To settle down within sea island sights,
Far from the beaten track in summer nights.

The time has come to lay my work aside,
And head down to my Island paradise.

Land's End

At land's end where shorelines begin,
The lighthouse stands proud, tall, and trim.
A structure of mortar, brick, or stone,
Out of the mist, it stands alone.

Imposing to the naked eye,
A giant stretching toward the sky,
Along coastlines and rocky shores,
The historical light reflects folklore.

From sailing ships in days of old,
Stories of pirates played and told,
A cast of light on swaggering waves,
Bows to time and yesterdays.

Today, folks come from far and wide
To get a glimpse of time and tides,
As on spiraling stairs they climb,
Step-by-step to view shorelines.

A gift shop now in the keeper's house
Portrays what history is all about.
Footfalls creak on random floors,
As tourists flow through salt sprayed doors.

Seashore treasures displayed on shelves,
Mementos of time and tidal swells.
The lighthouse shines through history,
A portal to maritime mysteries.

The light renewed on shifting sands,
Sometimes moved further inland,
To remain intact on seashore's brink,
And keep from collapse as seashores shrink.

Planted firmly on land's end sand,
Lighthouses dot the coastal strand;
Grand ghosts rising along our shores,
Calling, calling, forevermore.

Ocean's Lure

When ancient mariners sailed before,
And mermaids called forevermore,
Rolling across a sun-drenched sea,
The mermaids cried; "We sing for thee".

The haunting ocean's pristine lure
Knows what adventures lie in store
For one desiring to sail free
Across a green, enchanted, sea.

I'll leave my shoes on windblown sand
And take the wind by outreached hand;
Then race the shorelines splashed with surf
And catch the mermaids' songs of mirth.

I'll dip my big toe in green seas,
As mermaids gently call to me—
Sweet music blown on whispering waves
From darkest sea and shipwreck graves.

Sailing

Sailing on an ocean breeze,
Sandy toes, bare legged knees,
To lay my work-worn body down
On sandy beach with seaside sounds.

Gentle lapping of the deep,
Baby waves crawl; gently creep
Along a shoreline's graceful curve,
Sun splashed by swells that dip and swerve.

Sailing on in sunlight bright,
Through sunny days and seaside sights,
Beach umbrella is the mast
That hoists my dreams within my grasp.

Sailing on a dream within,
Sun rays slowly soak my skin,
Those warm my body with their touch,
That's all I ask, I don't want much.

Sailing on an ocean breeze
Billowing out from island keys,
As baby waves crawl; slowly creep
Across my feet while oceans sleep.

Salt Air

From deepest dregs of heart's despair,
Comes a call from salty air.
Gentle breezes blown from seas,
Tugging at the soul of me.

Salty air fresh, moist and fair,
By its sea winds takes me there.
Sea spray felt upon my skin,
Frees the tempest trapped within.

Salty air, fresh, warm and fair,
Ocean drops around my hair,
Crowning me like mermaids fair,
Reigning there by sea's salt air.

Seabird

As I feel the breeze from off the ocean,
Drops of salty air on suntan lotion,
I hear the waves break free upon the shore.
Through ocean time, the sea calls me once more.

Today begins anew when blue soaks through
My soul, the master of my ship and crew.
Immersed in beauty where blue sea meets sky,
In seaside mist, my life made new— baptized.

I am a seabird flying from the north,
Migrating southward, yearly, back and forth,
To navigate with compass of the heart,
Like Neptune, there are seas for me to chart.

Defined by frequent flights toward the south
To find the sound at yawning ocean's mouth,
An ocean paradise where seabirds flock,
Unbothered by the ticking of the clock.

When ancient mermaids first befriended me,
I promised to return back to the sea.
As seasons come and go, they call to me,
My journey must begin; I must sail free.

Starfish

Starfish, prickly starfish,
What is your wish?
To float upon the ocean floor
In a sea shell dish?

Starfish, little starfish,
Where do you float?
Over top the salty waves
In a sea shell boat?

I'll ride upon the ocean wave,
I'll ride upon the sea,
I'll ride upon a dolphin's back
If you should follow me.

Starfish, little starfish,
I'll make a wish on thee,
While riding on a dolphin's back
Like Neptune of the Sea.

And should my wish be granted,
I'll swim into the sea,
And catch another starfish wish
While you wade patiently!

Sweet Mermaid

Rise up, sweet mermaid, from your sleep,
Your secret mermaid dreams will keep.
Rise up from slumbering oceans deep
Where dancing waves play and leap.

Time to climb through sunbeams bright,
Up! Up! Up! To morning's light,
Ivory fingers through your hair
Flowing down in tresses fair.

Oh! What mysteries call to you?
From the deep, enchanted blue,
Safe within your underworld
Of swirling curls and white pearls.

Do you ever sneak a peek?
From coral beds in caves beneath?
Or, do you hide in castled sands
From prying eyes, defying man?

As I walk your timeless shores,
You call to me through folklore,
Your song hauntingly forlorn,
Blown like taps on ancient horns.

Weave for me your timeless tales
Of sailing ships and singing whales,
And mysteries of mystic seas,
Sweet mermaid, rendezvous with me.

The Beachcomber

My favorite place to be is by the sea,
To watch the golden sun rise from the east,
To see the morning mist play on the waves,
To walk along the beach my heart so craves.
Before the world awakes there are a few
Who gather treasures from the foamy dew,
Inspecting seashells washed upon the shore,
From oceans calling me, forevermore.
I am among the ranks, who comb the sands,
In early morning, digging with bare hands.
Each day I plan to gather but a few
Seashell treasures from the salty dew.
My favorite place to be is by the sea,
On the beach, my barefoot legacy,
To scan warm sands under golden skies;
I comb alone; yet, one with wind and tide.

The Light

Standing silent, weathered, worn,
On craggy cliffs through wintry storms,
Reaching arms of guiding light,
Shining hope through desperate nights.

The lighthouse braves torrential force,
Beaming over rocky course,
Watching, like a sentinel,
Dangers deep in ocean swells.

From the past its ghost appears,
A welcome host throughout long years,
Slowly slipped to disrepair,
Peering from its searching stare.

The keepers gone their lonely way,
A maddening death with time's decay.
Wearing harsh and haunting looks,
Weathered by time in history books.

The light and keeper fought the fight
Through sea sprayed days and stormy nights,
As courage marked a chosen few,
Who saved the bones of ship and crew.

Today, the lighthouse stands renewed
New generations are its glue,
Preserving once forgotten shores,
Through time and tide, light is restored.

The Jersey Shore

Hot summer day, take me away
    To the Oceanside where the seagulls play.
Bright summer sounds, time to take me down,
    Down to the beaches of the Jersey shore.

Walk along the boardwalk down in Wildwood,
    Hear the Jersey shore talk, on those planks of wood.
On Victorian walks over in old Cape May,
    Share Rita's water ice in the heat of day.

Stop at Mack and Manco's for a slice of pie,
    It's the shore's best pizza; what a tomato pie!
Stay across the Bay in good old Ocean City,
    Use the outdoor shower so you won't feel gritty!

A summer wind is blowing; everybody's going,
    To the sandy beaches of the Jersey shore.
You couldn't ask for more; find out what's in store
    When you spend your summer at the New Jersey shore.

The Oyster

'Twas long ago when I crawled from the sea
And grew land legs in support of me.
I vaguely recall the sea splashing 'round,
White capped waves with tempo and sound.

Rolling, rocking, rhythm pushing me along,
And sweet melodies of fair mermaids' songs.
Oceans and centuries passed through my hands,
As I crawled from the sea to the white, virgin sands.

Long ago, eons ago, through the pull of the moon,
I came with support of a heartbeat in tune,
Emerging like a creature from a sleepy lagoon
To break like a wave from the pull of that moon.

I hardly recall growing fingers and toes,
When I crawled from the deep, no one truly knows,
But the secret was placed by the sea in my heart,
To remain there forever, calling me from the start.

The voice of the deep forever keeps calling
Back to the cradle from which I came crawling,
"I am your Mother, your Father, who guarded your sleep,
When the world was your oyster in the sweet watery deep."

The Sea

When I am by the sea, I am made free
To hear the calling straight from God to me.
I am as one with nature, wind, and sky,
My hopes and dreams released to fly so high.

The human light is trapped as in a shell
Of flesh and bones caught up by worldly spells;
Released like waves broke free from passing tides,
Renewed with time spent by the ocean side.

The truth of all I am lives by the sea,
With every white capped wave that comes to be,
Returning to its source eternally,
Through time and tide to form its destiny.

The way the morning light spreads 'cross the sky
Is living proof God creates on high,
He makes the sunrise in a painted sky,
In perfect harmony as time goes by.

God teaches me we're branches of His light,
Providing seas and scenes of which to write,
His signature is seen in glorious skies,
With every sunrise painted for my eyes.

Believing in creation is the key,
That frees the truth of life eternally.
When man with God is willing to agree,
The human light will seek its destiny.

I love this life that God has granted me,
Rejuvenated by tides, by wind, by sea,
Reminded of the life He breathes in me—
Each time a wave returns back to the sea.

The Sea Shell

The sea shell is a pretty thing
From which sea creatures slowly spring,
To find another space to dwell
Beneath the tide and ocean's swell.

A captivating work of art,
The sea shell speaks to seaward hearts.
This precious jewel began its start
'Neath leagues of seas in brackish dark.

The sea shell's color, texture and size,
Its shape and feel, a treasured prize,
Which holds the ocean in its sound,
Old worlds and seas within abound.

The Shell is found in hues of pink,
Tumbling over in oceans' drink,
Beautiful tones in sea grown hues,
With splashes of blue sifting through.

The sea shell travels space and time
And charts the seas as one of a kind;
A worthy gift from oceans deep,
A treasured prize for those who seek.

The sea shell is a pretty thing,
More prized than gold of captain or king.
For those who own a seaward heart,
The sea shell is a work of art.

SUMMERTIME

Summertime brings wings to the heart...

Lost in Sunshine

I shall get lost in the sunshine today,
Time to shed old trappings of yesterday.
Roses are sweet with the scent of the bloom,
I'll skip through the meadow; my heart in tune.

I think I'll get lost in green grass and clover,
Where honey bees buzz, I'll take my cover.
I shall get lost in wildflowers and clover,
Barefoot in sweet grass until summer's over.

I shall stroll by the stream, lost in my thoughts,
Stepping on big rocks should I wish to cross.
If I should slip and fall in up to my chin,
I'll dry off with sunshine and warm my skin.

I want to get lost where the tall grass grows,
Where daisies grow high; where nobody mows.
Rather than not, I'll lie by an old tree,
And watch clouds drifting in blue skies above me.

I want to get lost where cool waters flow,
Searching for flat rocks to skip a stone's throw.
If I have my way, I'll throw stones all day,
I'll be an expert rock skipper today.

I might feel brave and climb the apple tree,
And pick a plump apple, red, ripe, and juicy.
If I should hang upside down from a branch,
I'll hold on with my knees when I take that chance.

I think I'll get lost in warm summertime,
Drink lemonade, fresh, that would be very fine.
I might bring my friend to get lost with me,
With her tail wagging we both will roam free.

If you should desire to get lost with me,
Leave your knapsack behind, hung on a tree.
There is no need for thoughts of yesterday,
When we go get lost in sunshine today.

Thoughts of Summertime

Sunny weather,
   Sparrow feathers,
Outdoor fountains,
   Moonlit mountains.

Garden flags,
   Flower tags,
Daffodils,
   Green grass hills.

Watering holes,
   Fishing poles,
Slow and lazy,
   Sunshine hazy.

Summer breeze,
   Sunlit knees,
Buzzing bees,
   Firefly memories,

Summertime…

Wings of the Heart

Springtime gives birth to summer,
And summertime brings wings to the heart.

Summertime is:

A time when nature wears her perfume,
A time when butterflies shed their cocoons,
A time for sand crabs to leave their shells,
A time for long walks by wishing wells,
A time for people to leave their rooms,
A time when the earth is covered in blooms,
A time to hear two love doves croon,
A time for fireflies and silvery moons,
A time to dine with plastic forks and spoons.

Sunshine warms the skin as summer's glow begins…

A time to dive and take a swim,
When water is warm; time to jump in,
Time to pack a picnic lunch,
Time to relax, sit back and munch.
A time when cornfields grow sky-high,
A time when flying fish catch the eye,
A time when fishermen catch the prize,
And delight in casting the fly.

Summertime brings gladness to the heart…

A time for long strolls in the park,
A time to stay up late, well after dark,
A time for sandaled suntanned feet,
To slowly walk through summer's heat.
A time for vacation's standing ovation,
A time for high school graduation,
A time for lightening bugs in jars,
A time to wish on a twinkling star.

Summertime brings wings to the heart…

A time for hometown celebrations and parades,
A time for drinking fresh squeezed lemonade,
A time when baseball games are played,
A time when strawberry shortcake is made.
A time for running after the ice cream man,
A time when family cookouts are planned.
A time for walks to the water ice stand,
A time for lovers and holding hands,
A time for building castles in the sand!

A time for toasting marshmallows and roasting sweet corn,
A time when the spirit is rejuvenated and reborn.
A time for sail boating out on the lake,
A time for bonfires, lobster and clambakes,
A time to cool down in the old swimming hole,
A time to catch frogs, toads and tadpoles.
A time to sing around campfires after dark;
All of these things bring wings to the heart.

Summertime is a time to visit with friends
Until summer ends
Until next year when summertime mends,
We'll do it all over again.

THE INNER CHILD

Call the child that was left back there,
The child with the wind-blown hair...

A Distant Sunbeam

There lives a distant sunbeam
Peeking through my memories,
Lighting up a wondrous dream
From far away on a shimmering sea.

There rests a glistening drop of dew,
Gleaming where the tall grass grew,
Calling a child I once knew,
Singing sweet songs in the meadow for you.

Grown in a field, dandelion weeds,
Blown on winds from little seeds,
A young child pulls a buttercup in,
Reflecting its light on another's chin.

Perchance to chase a butterfly
With silky wings to fly up high;
Perchance to catch a drifting dragonfly,
Or to launch a kite with one easy try.

There shines your own personal star,
Sparkling over that land afar,
Reach out; catch your very own dream,
Waiting for you on a blue moonbeam.

Call the child that was left back there,
The child with the wind-blown hair.
Run through the rays of the distant sun,
You are that child; time to become one.

Here in My Heart

I've reached out for the child within,
And I've taken her in
From the memories of sunlight
Dancing on her skin.

I've looked back to the days
Where this little girl played,
Outback in the yard,
And I've asked her to stay.

Here in my heart,
I'm holding the small hands
That made the mud pies
Near the lemonade stand.

Chattering voices—
    Little girl friends
Digging in the earth,
Mixing mud pies with pretend.

I'm holding the hand
Of that fine little girl,
As we run through the landscape
That we both know so well.

I'm right at home here in my heart
Holding the child within in my memories;
At home playing in an apple-green park,
Or barefoot in fields of wild strawberries.

I'm right at home now that I've grown,
While all these years I've known
Her happiness to be simple and pure,
Sunday's child has knocked on my door.

I'll not let go of this little girl's hands,
Now I've found her, she is where I am.

Rainbows

Love blends the colors of your own rainbow
Healing and guiding wherever you go.
I see you within a crystal clear dream
Walking the banks of your life's endless stream.

You have trodden a road where I cannot go,
Searching for truth and your personal rainbow.
When you feel your life might burst at the seams,
Keep your eye on the prize; follow your dreams.

One foot before the other, one step at a time,
You will find your rhythm and your personal rhyme.
Dreams live not in the mind but in the depths of the heart,
Follow your dream that you've known from the start.

Believing in God is your anchor in the wind,
Leave dark thoughts outside; do not let them in.
With all that you do, "to thine own self be true",
Knowing patience is a blessing and a true virtue.

All things in life will one day come to pass,
When time slips like sand through the hourglass.
Future plans will be made whenever you're ready,
Meanwhile, the mast of each day must be kept steady.

Emotions are like horses; they need to be tamed,
Leave them not unattended on life's rough terrain.
Open your feelings, one at a time,
Be gentle; walk softly, one step-at-a-time.

Your inner child wants to come out and play,
Calmly, take his hand and love him today.
Treat him with kindness, love and respect,
Enable your heart with his to connect.

A bridge may be built with caring and love,
Your inner child waits in your heart for your hug
Waiting and wanting to be held in your arms,
To be loved and protected and kept safe from harm.

Love him and hug him and tell him your thoughts,
Hold him closely as life's lessons are taught.
Under the bridge made of love's awesome rainbow,
Your child within waits for your truth, you know.

Should your child within cry, comfort him today,
Kiss away the tears of lost yesterdays.
Once you have found him, never let him go,
Come to know the truth of love's bright rainbow.

The Child Within

On great plumpy pillows of fantasy,
In goose down feathers, my memories;
Singing on swings of childlike wisdom,
Catching bright stars in a magical prism.

Sunset falling on yesterday's dreams,
A crazy Mad Hatter and quarreling queens.
Chasing, with Alice, an ageless March Hare,
Tumbling through tunnels—
    A white rabbit's lair.

Memories are keys to the tinkling of time,
Turning to nine with each passage of rhyme,
The child within waving a gold timeless torch,
Venturing through volumes
    On a creaky old porch.

WINGS

Wings of wisdom fly through time
Like guardians from the light....

My Angel, Treesah

Follow the path of your angel dear,
She understands your deepest fear,
Your guide for life, she lives in light,
A bearer of love, just out of sight.

Flying on wings of the morning dove,
Straight to your heart from God's love,
Showing you secrets she wants you to see,
Sitting beside you, she'll let you be.

She prompts you so you'll understand,
She moves your heart and guides your hand.
In silent whispers, she speaks to you,
Until you know what you must do.

An angel creates the things you love,
Just what your dreams are made of,
Her smile the sun in morning skies,
As she walks in the light of your eye.

Treesah, my guardian angel's name,
Falls like dew in sunshine's rain,
Gathering streams of sparking light,
Bursting forth in brilliant white light.

My angel slips into my dreams,
Under cover of pale moonbeams,
She patiently waits to see me rise,
To heed her call; to hear her sighs.

She resonates like musical notes,
Lighter than air, around me, she floats,
In harmony she guides my hand,
That plays the strings of my own band.

All things in life have rhythm and rhyme,
Nature is filled with a tempo sublime.
All God's creation walks His line,
Playing His drum, one beat at a time.

My angel keeps perfect harmony,
In tune with the task of letting me be me.
The best things in this life are free,
This truth my angel tells me.

My angel is love; she guides me through,
She knows exactly what I must do.
The truth of what is best for me,
When I make time to follow her lead.

Dearest angel, guardian dear,
You fill my time; you keep me near,
Bringing me peace as I sit here,
A gift of love when you appear.

My Reverie

When in my silent reverie
Shadows speak and part the seas,
And Holy Spirit sits with me.
Directing my every thought and deed.

When in my unborn thoughts, I write,
From early morn to darkest night,
A band of angels from above
Brings to me the Master's love.

'Tis He that holds my hand so firm
Giving birth to thoughts and words.
Whose ideas have come home to me?
If not He who writes my destiny.

When in the morning's light, I rise,
And wipe the sleep from my eyes,
Angels watch from near my side,
Planting seeds soon to arise.

Beautiful verses come to me,
As the good Lord helps me see.
As if across a vast expanse,
Meaning springs from happenstance.

Daily, Spirit summons me
From deep within my reverie,
The angels speak of glorious things,
Of beautiful light in glowing rings.

A band of angels hover 'round;
They sing to me; I hear their sounds.
A sweet but silent chorus made
By angels singing on parade.

They swoop and swirl;
They glide and twirl,
Lovely are the dreams they hide,
Under white wings, soft and wide.

Around my head, I feel them now,
As they cross soft puffy clouds.
Whispering words so I can hear,
They put their sweet lips to my ear.

When in the longest time of day,
God's angels come and take me away,
To a quiet place of golden verse,
Where God creates my universe.

Believe me now, for I have seen
God's angels who have filled my dreams.
I fear not dark or evil ways,
For He has sent his angels today.

Hanging onto their every word,
I fly on wings of words I heard,
Discovering a vast expanse of land,
Void of cities and slums of man.

Son of Man is Son of God.
This truth has blown through wind and fog,
The truth is my reality,
God is love; He sets me free.

Oh! Write until your heart's content,
This is the truth the angels sent,
They watch me as I go to sleep,
Through the night, my dreams, they keep.

Tomorrow when I rise again,
Angels whisper; I write again,
Recalling a bright reality
When angel's wisdom comes to me.

Reflections Through Time and Rhyme

I must express my thankfulness
To my angel who brings me bliss.
She plucks a topic from the sky,
And floats it down before my eyes.

When in and out of thought, I step,
I am unaware if my angel has left;
Yet, her energy stays around awhile,
And creates my mood and writing style.

Write on freedom, or write on love,
It's all the same to God above.
In heaven the best is yet to be,
When angels serve humility.

Time to go to bed and sleep,
All my cares and worries will keep.
Misty morn draws nigh to me,
With loving angels sent from thee.

When in my quiet reverie,
Vibrations flow like light to me,
Angels stream from light afar,
While my dreams fly me to the stars.

The Calling

No one knows my secret heart,
Not even I can see,
The priceless pearls beneath the dark
    Waves of destiny.

As I write, my spirit knows
The workings of my soul,
Harvesting words so sweetly blown
    Through wheat fields in times of old.

The mind is like a well-built dam
With floodgates closed up tight.
The watchman walks with outreached hand
    To flood the heart with light.

Wings of wisdom fly through time,
Like guardians from the light,
Clearing whirlwinds from my mind,
    Dusting my eyes with sight.

Sitting in my room alone,
I am not alone at all.
The winds have blown, once more shown,
    Inscriptions on the wall.

I know not what the guardians see,
Yet, one fact I know for sure,
Wherever the port I am meant to be,
    I will light upon its shore.

The Poetry Angel

The poetry angel speaks to me
In pretty prose and poetry.
Sweet little words so soft and clear
When angel whispers in my ear.

I never know what words she'll speak,
When she searches my heart and sneaks a peek.
But she finds emotions inside my soul
And spins them with words etched in gold.

My angel bids me to take up my pen,
To write on paper, secrets treasured within.
For a moment I see through my angel's eyes,
Fluffy powder puff moons in star bright skies.

A ribbon of gold connects angel's wings
To my world of paper and heartstrings.
Softly, she tugs, and I write the rhyme,
My heart grows wings and begins its climb.

Through the Shadows

Through the shadows of my heart,
Diamonds sparkle in the dark,
Where a treasure chest unopened
Holds lovely words unspoken.

Through the halls and labyrinths,
Walk the pathways of silent footprints
Leading on to an open door,
Where diamonds shine forevermore.

There is a glistening masterpiece
Springing to life with signs of peace,
And harmonies yet unsung,
Like doves waiting to be sprung.

Inside my mind lives a spirit
Bringing wisdom when I'm near it,
Creating scenes that flow and spout;
The stuff writing is about.

There's an angel within my soul
Painting a sunrise to behold,
To silent whispers I am drawn,
Lovely words are my life's song.

Through the shadows of my heart,
Diamonds shine and sparkle in the dark,
Where a treasure yet to be given,
Is a measure yet unwritten.

Velvet angels white and blue,
Among the dusty shadows flew,
Bringing sight with signature light,
As I sit down, quietly, and write.

Pretty pictures in my mind,
Like white diamonds dazzle and shine,
Where angels write upon the walls
And hallways, where the shadows fall.

Within my heart, within my mind,
There's an exquisite diamond mine,
Among the shadows where the doves fly—
    A haven where diamonds shine
        Like stars in a seamless velvet sky.

Velvet Wings

Velvet wings in airy skies,
Feathered as they fly up high.
Graceful, gloriously gliding by,
Beautiful wings in flight on high.

Soaring upward, wingspans wide,
Turning, gliding, side-to-side,
Hawk eyes searching, circle round,
Victims captured make no sound.

Hunts on high dare not retreat,
Keen eyes seek out tempting treats.
Higher than kites, ink wings fly,
Cutting through a cloudless sky.

Jet-black flights in skies of blue
Velvet wings, a beautiful view,
With ease of flight, power, might
Black wings climb as dark as night.

WINTERTIME

I remember winter,
Knee-deep with snow…

A Candle's Light

A candle's light shines in the window, bright,
Reaching through the dark and wintry storm,
A beacon holding heart and home in warmth,
While spreading light on pathways dark at night.

Forge on, Oh! Weary traveler through the night,
A little flame gleams to light your way,
To lead you from your rough and trying day,
To guide you to warm shelter with its sight.

A candle's flame is worth one hundred words,
As its beauty beams from up the lane,
Shining its message for the shepherd's herd,
Showing home is through the window's pane.

A candle spreads its light from lantern's glow,
On countryside and pastures by the way,
On village shires steeped in deepest snow,
Shining its truth to end the longest day.

Bless Our Mountain Home

Bless this, our lovely mountain home,
Where forest creatures love to roam.
Among white pines and evergreen,
Beside clear sparkling mountain streams.

May this good place inspire you,
To fish from lake; boat, or canoe,
By misty mountains looming high
Into the blue-white mountain sky.

Whether log cabin or chalet,
Bless this, our mountain home today.
May it withstand winter's deep snows;
Warm summers when lake waters glow.

Bless our beautiful mountain home,
The fireside, the chimney stone.

Ice Skating Memories

Down on the pond frozen over with ice,
We'll put on our skates; circle around twice,
Carry ice skates; tie up the laces,
Wave to the neighbors with rosy red faces.

Winter has come; frosty air stings our noses,
Out on the pond in ice-skating poses,
Scarves bundled round our cheeks of red roses,
Last night the pond water froze!

Joyfully, Dad skates and makes figure eights,
As he slides his feet on the ice.
Dad spins me around, maybe once, maybe twice,
My Dad looks good on the ice.

I see Dad and me in my memory,
Skating with hearts young and carefree.
With love in my heart, clearly, I see
Dad following me, as he warmly agrees…

To carry my skates and tie up the laces,
And make figure eights, leaving his traces,
In winters alive with wind-kissed faces–
In winters gone by on the pond.

Snow Day

Making snow angels and snowmen from snowflakes,
Sledding down hillsides alongside a white lake,
Catching snowflakes on the tip of your tongue,
Makes you feel, Oh, so young!

Walking in snow drifts up to your kneecaps,
Donning your warm boots, mittens and wool hats,
Pulling a child on a red runner sled,
On snow day; get out of bed!

Building a snowman out in the front yard,
Rolling round snowballs is easy; it's not hard,
Take a snapshot of your pure handiwork,
    Turn on the news; there's a snow alert!

Making snow angels and snowmen from snowflakes,
"Get up and go" is the only thing it takes
For pulling a child on a red runner sled,
Today is a snow day; get out of bed!

Catching snowflakes
    On the tip of your tongue
        Makes one feel, Oh, so young!

The Big If
Home of Dreams

If I could hole up in my home
      And write upon the walls,
I'd write for sanity alone
      Until spring weather calls.

I'd paint, like Michael Angelo,
      The ceiling with my brush,
In colors bold with golden glow
      On wide fields, sage and lush.

I'd take my pen with sparkling ink,
      Creating waterfalls,
And blooming roses climbing pink,
      Inscribed on every wall.

I'd fill my hours with brilliant light,
      Like Tutankhamen's gold.
I'd pull down diamonds from the night
      For my eyes to behold.

I would be taken by God's gift
      These gloriously glowing scenes.
His work would give my heart a lift;
      My home filled with His dreams.

We'll All Wear Hats

Winter's deep snow has forced our hands indoors
To occupy our time with twiddling thumbs,
And making beds and sweeping up our crumbs
Behind closed doors to scrub our snow tracked floors.

Our mundane lives are broken by small chores;
While peeking through glass panes for fading suns,
And growing fat consuming hot cross buns,
Searching for ways to keep from being bored.

Here in the north while winter has its way,
Our cash is burned and turned to heat for homes,
Preventing walls from turning cold as stones,
Keeping outside old winter's wrath at bay.

When venturing out of doors, we'll all wear hats,
Donning snow boots for treading on thin ice.
Waiting for summer's sun, we'll pay the price,
Amusing self with battening down the hatch.

As winter bares his teeth, we'll all wear hats,
Bolting the latch while pulling down our flaps!

Winter

I remember winter, knee-deep with snow,
And blankets of white over hill and meadow.
Icicles dripping like crystals from rooflines,
Wonderland miracles frozen in time.

I remember snowmen, round, jolly and fat,
Dressed in plaid flannel and old tattered hat.
I remember flying on red sleds down snow hills,
And small fingers stinging from winter's cold chill.

Cups of hot chocolate with spongy marshmallows,
Steaming and hot; warm right down to the toes,
And red boots, and snowsuits, brown moose,
And the wonderful feeling of being footloose.

Epilogue

Let us fly away to the meadow,
With its bright sunbeams at play,
Dancing like children's shadows,
On a perfect sunlit day.

We shall visit Christopher Robin,
Share a spot of honey with Pooh,
Or sneak a peek at a Hobbit
Walking in pointed shoes.

We shall leave behind the old world
And civilized pursuits,
At heart we are as young girls
Putting our dreams to good use.

Good day again, my dear friend,
I shall take a moment or two,
And discover the end of the rainbow's bend
And happily walk with you.

www.ingramcontent.com/pod-product-compliance
Lightning Source LLC
Chambersburg PA
CBHW022016090426
42739CB00006BA/160